Business Tips
From
The Trenches

Expert Advice to Start Your Small Business or Side Hustle

Ira Bowman and Joel Phillips

Janet Hogan, Dr. Andrea Renee Rivera,
Tonia Stoney, Will Kralovec, Danila
Palmieri, Tia Cristy, Tonya Baynes,
Dionne Tuplin, Shawn Huber

ISBN: 979-8-89079-032-3 (paperback)

ISBN: 978-1-64184-995-1 (hardback)

ISBN: 978-1-64184-996-8 (ebook)

TABLE OF CONTENTS

EXPANDED
TABLE OF CONTENTS

PREFACE

I didn't seek to become a business owner, let alone a full-fledged entrepreneur. However, that is precisely where I have found myself over the past three years. I transitioned from an employee to a business owner one weekend after being laid off (from a job I thought I would retire from) due to the COVID-19 pandemic and its devastating effect on the hospitality industry here in Southern California.

Some of the best things that can happen to us in life come on the heels of what we think at the time is bad news or an unlucky break. Much of life is perspective and how we look at it. I remember being gripped by the fear of not knowing how I would support my family. I don't have a master's degree in business and didn't have experience running a company. However, I did have some experience in sales, marketing, and management, and that, coupled with a large LinkedIn following of 150,000 followers (at the time), gave me enough confidence in my skills that I could make a small business successful if I ran it lean and focused on helping other small business owners increase their visibility on LinkedIn to help drive sales. I launched Bowman Digital Media on a shoestring budget (I only had $12,000 in the bank) on prayer and faith in my abilities.

Are you looking to start your own business? In this book, some of my small-business-owner friends and I share tips and lessons learned from our experience that will help you avoid some of the mistakes we made. Our goal is simple—we want to help you! In each chapter, you'll find three tips and one thing we wish we could have done better. These lessons will help you accomplish your goals faster if you apply them.

Let me encourage you first with just a few thoughts from the thousands of business owners I've talked to over the years.

1. No one has all the answers, so don't wait to start until you have figured it all out.

2. Run your business on a solid business plan that has been vetted by someone who knows the industry you will get into. There is great wisdom in listening to others who have gone before you.

3. Your closest friends and family might not fully support you initially, as they might need time to adjust to your new reality.

4. Don't forget to make time for yourself, your family, and some outside hobby, or you'll fall apart much faster than you think.

5. Don't try to do everything yourself. If you want to go fast, go alone; if you want to go far, go with a team.

Too many small businesses fail because the owner doesn't get the help they need; they run out of money because of a lack of sales or ruin their reputation by biting off more than they can chew.

You were smart enough to pick up this book. You can absorb the many lessons here and even more as you start your journey. It can be a lonely road filled with late nights. You will make mistakes because you are human. No one in this book will ever judge you because of your mistakes. I encourage you with the news that mistakes help us learn if we allow them to. So buckle up and keep reading. We have a lot to share, and I'm excited for you to get insight I wish I had sought out before starting my business ownership journey. One final thought—I've never been happier or had more financial independence than I do right now. Being a business owner has been an incredible journey, filled with struggles, hard times, unexplainable joy, and pride from seeing my logo next to many cool projects. I can't wait for you to get that same experience as you continue pursuing your new business venture.

—Ira Bowman

FOREWORD BY GEORGE JONES

The excitement, fear, and risk that come with pursuing your dream can be an adrenaline rush, and it will take you to your deepest points. Regardless of the outcome, perseverance, vulnerability, transparency, and a great support system will see you through.

I grew up in the projects of Greenville, South Carolina. My mom has a seventh-grade education, and she did the best that she could. She was not around much, either. I would experience extreme poverty, abuse, and homelessness. My grades suffered, which meant no offers for a college scholarship to play football. My surrogate dad, Monnie Broome, would connect me to the best football program in the country at a community college. It was across the country in Bakersfield, California.

With excitement, fear, and risk, I boarded Delta Flight 93 and made the trip. I had two successful years at Bakersfield Community College and went on to play at San Diego State University. I became part of the 1% and be drafted into the NFL by the Pittsburgh Steelers. I experienced the rush of the crowd, what it felt like for a coach to tell me I was cut from the team, and a doctor telling me it was in my best interest to retire my cleats. Many people tell me it was an experience they dreamed of.

But it turns out that wasn't my dream. I wanted to be a dad. A dad who would be there every step of the way. To be the dad I didn't have growing up—the dad I have never known.

Much like football, my fatherhood journey has had its up and downs. I approached fatherhood much like football. I thought I was raising an athlete. I coached all his sports. I was hard on him at a very young age, and I expected perfection. It was not until my wife filmed me coaching a game and I saw how manic I was on the field that I knew I had to make changes. To be the best father I can be, I had to ask for help. I had to get mentors.

I watched the documentary *The Manning Story* a film about Archie Manning and his three sons, Cooper, Peyton, and Eli. It shows his fatherhood journey, and his relationship with his boys struck me.

I contacted Archie, who has since become my mentor. I called every man I knew who was a father, regardless of their race or background, men I respected and perceived as good fathers, and I asked for their advice. I asked what worked well for them, and what their mistakes were. I knew I was not being the best father I could be, and my boys deserved better.

I thought about other fathers I had observed throughout my life and thought about what being a Present Dad looked like. For me, sure, I was with them 24/7, but I was not *with*; I was not truly present. Through these conversations with men nationwide, I realized I was not the only man wanting help to be a better father. I created The Present Dad Foundation, where we work to help dads be genuinely present with their kids. I wrote a book, and now I am an international bestselling author.

As you read *Business Tips From The Trenches*, I hope you will soak up the incredible lessons from the journeys included. They are rooted in perseverance, vulnerability, and transparency. Their courage led them to take that first step, and I hope you will, too.

IRA BOWMAN

Tip 1: If you spend all your time working in your business, you won't have time to build it

Grow your team as fast as possible. That might seem impossible initially, especially if you are working on a shoestring budget, commonly referred to as bootstrapping these days. I get it. I started my business with $12,000 in the bank, but my monthly expenses were just over $6,000 per month to provide for my family of nine here in Southern California. Trust me when I tell you I know what it's like to pinch pennies. I started Bowman Digital Media for $3,000 after filing for my LLC, getting a new computer, and buying some necessary software to operate my business. That left me with enough cash on hand to pay the bills for six weeks. However, working alone, I was able to generate enough revenue that I didn't have to touch that reserve cash as I ran my business lean and only bought extra things from the profit that my sales generated.

In full disclosure, I generated over $100,000 in sales my first year. That's not bad for a one-man band. You might think this was a good thing, but I wonder how much more I could have accomplished if I had brought a team in sooner. You see, there's an opportunity cost (a high one) for running sixteen-hour days, six days a week. I ignored my family, my health, and everything not business related to get there. (I revisit this later in this chapter.)

In my second year, I wised up. I figured out that, even though I could not afford full-time W2 employees, I could hire 1099 labor, especially offshore labor. I received much-needed help so I could focus on sales, work on the business vision, add new services, and market via podcast appearances, TEDx Talks, attend training sessions, and more. The results were great, and I had more free time to do other things.

About eighteen months into my business, after attending a training seminar, I learned about internship programs, which really improved my business. It truly is brilliant. I started trading my knowledge, in the form of training, in exchange for free labor brought into my company by interns (including kids fresh out of school and more experienced professionals looking to switch industries) who wanted to break into the digital marketing space. In my program, the intern provides ten hours of their time working for me in exchange for one hour of me training them on a specific marketing skill like design, SEO, or social media. It also helps me identify great talent, like an extended job interview for the best interns, so I no longer have trouble deciding who to bring on as W2 labor.

You can go fast and go far. I suggest you build your team and get the help you need ASAP.

Tip 2: Being obscure is bad; do not ignore marketing and SEO

One of new business owners' most significant mistakes is trying to monetize right out of the gate. Why is this a problem? Mainly because you don't have enough visibility to fill your sales funnel properly, and you lose heart, waste money on stagnant inventory, and run out of cash. Cash is king, so you must consider how to generate leads in a volume that can sustain your business. The best traffic generator on the planet right now is Google. There are 81,000 searches on average every second of every day on Google.

Do you have a Google strategy? If the answer is no—and that's probably true for most of you—seek an organic SEO strategist to help you. You want to build your website out in an SEO-optimized fashion and work hard to build the SERP (search engine results page) position of your website right away. You want to look at keywords and the types of volumes associated with them on Google so you can produce content that answers those questions. You want to have video content on all your website pages for visitors to consume once they land on your site.

Don't ignore social media, either. True masters of the game don't play to their personal preferences; they build strategies based on the psychographics and demographics of their target clients. If you love LinkedIn, but your target audience is on Instagram and Twitter, you'd be foolish to ignore those platforms. Just because your business is new doesn't mean you can't utilize existing marketing data to develop a comprehensive strategy based on pre-existing data.

Other beneficial things you can do to increase your visibility include being a podcast guest, writing a book or contributing as a co-author to a book, contributing to guest blogs, putting out a press release, speaking as a speaker at live events, giving a TEDx talk, sponsoring local events (where your target market participants will be), paying for article placements in magazines like Forbes, joining networking groups, and writing articles on platforms like LinkedIn and Medium.

Don't die on the vine and watch your dreams go up in flames because you failed to increase both your business and personal visibility.

Tip 3: Schedule time for life, including time for your family, dating your significant other, exercising, sleeping, and reading

"You can't pour from an empty cup" is a popular expression for a reason. If you don't make time to take care of yourself and the ones you love, why are you doing all of this for? Far too many of us who start businesses lose sight of that fact. I am guilty, for sure. Sixteen-hour days, six or seven days a week, might make you think you're killing it, but you're just killing everything around you. Danger! It's a trap, fool's gold, and the price tag is far higher than you can imagine. So how do you make time? Reread my first tip. I gave you two viable options for getting inexpensive or free labor to help you with this most important tip.

How do you budget your time? I love to work off of a block schedule. I have time set aside for walks, lunch, dinner, reading, writing, dating my wife, church, networking, internal team meetings, external client meetings, photography, and more. The bottom line is, if it's not on my schedule, I likely won't do it. The biggest thing is setting the time blocks and then sticking to them. Get an accountability partner to help you if you need it as you adjust. If you try to run your time ad-hock, you will waste far more time doing things that don't matter. I call that letting the tail wag the dog. A block schedule might feel constrictive at first, but it's just like a fiscal budget in that it frees you to guilt-free spend the time as designated in the time blocks.

Lesson Learned: Don't over-focus on what your prospects and clients need instead, build around what they want that your product or service can deliver

Sales and momentum depend on sharing what people are interested in buying, not selling them on what you believe they need. Yes, I know that the two are the same in some cases, but most of the time, you'll find it isn't.

Have you ever heard the saying, "What happens in Vegas, stays in Vegas?"

Las Vegas is a place people go to have a good time. They generally go to experience what they want, not what they need—staying up late, drinking too much, gambling, seeing exotic shows, and a host of other things they may or may not want anyone to know about. Many will have the "time of their life," and drop *a lot* of money on it. Why? Because it's what they want. Love or hate Las Vegas, there are great lessons to be learned from how the town has grown into a major metropolis. They even have professional sports teams now because of how they market the Vegas experience. As a child from Vegas, I should have learned some of these lessons long ago, but I didn't.

Let's dive into the main lesson in detail now—focus on the wants, not the needs, especially when trying to ramp up your client base.

Don't like Vegas? No worries, here's another analogy that you can digest easier. How many know that fruits and vegetables are healthier than candy? Drinking juice and milk is generally healthier than drinking soda or adult beverages. If you open your refrigerator, what are you more likely to see? Are you going to find healthy foods and drinks or things that are sugar or alcohol filled? While many like to talk about being healthy, most people are more likely to purchase non-healthy food and drinks. This is an excellent lesson for us to remember when we communicate with our prospects and clients about what we do, how we help, and how they might benefit.

When I launched Bowman Digital Media, I had specific ways to help people increase their visibility on social media and Google. However, I struggled to get the masses to listen, even though it was what they needed, because I didn't focus on what they wanted. My messaging was not built for success.

Here's the lesson. Observe your target market and learn about what they want. Once you understand what they want, you can start to craft your marketing and sales materials around those. For me, my target market is looking to increase top-line sales. My original message of increasing visibility online or driving more organic website traffic was simply missing the mark because my audience wasn't making the connection, I thought they would. I was working under the assumption that people would understand that higher-visibility online and more website traffic would translate into higher sales. This was faulty and cost me time and sales and caused needless frustration.

So, what did I do? I listened carefully to what the audience I was chasing had to say. Most were talking about their desire to increase revenue and drive sales. I got to work asking more questions about their wants to help formulate new marketing materials and rephrasing things on my website.

I also learned from these conversations and observations that many saw the work we offered as costly overhead and not revenue generators, when in fact, SEO, social media posts, and website work can be one of the highest revenue vehicles available. The work to transition wasn't originally on my radar, but it was needed if I was going to drive more sales and effectively help more clients at Bowman Digital Media.

After hearing what people wanted, I reformulated my website. I changed the message on the homepage of my website, reworded the package offers on my service pages, and put out a new message on social media. People wanted more sales, so I talked how SEO and social media can generate a lot more sales by bringing in new prospects to businesses that utilize our services. I also asked clients to provide referrals on how our services helped them drive sales.

I'm not saying you should only focus on pleasure or things that are not good for your future clients. I'm saying that in most cases, if you focus on what they want and show them how it can also benefit them, sales will happen much faster, making your job easier. If you listen to what the crowd you're chasing wants, and create campaigns around how you can deliver it, that is an easy-to-digest message.

In my case, people want to increase their sales, and the products and services I offer don't change. We've offered the same six services at Bowman Digital Media since I launched the business in June 2020. The change I made that helped me catch the prospect's attention was in the terminology I used. I found ways to say how SEO (being at the top of Google) and our other services would help them increase sales.

Do you want a practical example of how I specifically changed my message?

At the top of my website, it used to say: Increase Your Visibility Online. We Help Drive Organic Traffic to Your Website Without Paying for Expensive Ads.

Now, at the top of my website, it says: Need More Sales? Want to Rank Higher on Google? We Help Drive More of the Right Visitors to Our Client's Websites to Increase Their Sales.

The methods we utilized to do this didn't change. However, the new message resonates much better with our target audience. They understand what we can do for them, which appeals to their wants. They need the SEO, social media, and website help they always did; they just didn't understand how our services delivered what they were looking for.

The rest of the messaging on my website has been rewritten to help support the message that our services help our clients increase their sales.

What do you do now that you know you must focus on the prospect's wants instead of talking about what they need? First, diagnose what they want. Then, go back to the drawing board and see which of your messages are missing that mark and rewrite them. You might need to hire a branding or marketing professional to help with this.

One surefire way to ensure your message is on point is to conduct prospect and customer surveys. Ask questions about what they are trying to do. Ask how they are currently trying to accomplish their goals. Ask what roadblocks are slowing them down or stopping them from succeeding.

Once you have the data in hand, you can more easily recraft the messaging on your website and in your email campaigns, along with the wording you're using on social media to catch their attention. Stop selling based on need. Start focusing on language that resonates with what your prospects want. It will help you sell more and sell faster. It certainly has made a world of difference for my team at Bowman Digital Media, and we are continuing to grow both in size and revenue because of it.

ABOUT THE AUTHOR

Professionally Ira is a marketing and sales expert, photographer, graphics designer, website builder, philanthropy owner, Search Engine Optimization content writer, published author, and TEDx speaker.

Ira Bowman holds a Bachelor of Science degree from Liberty University, where he graduated with a 3.916 GPA in Interdisciplinary Studies, with a concentration in Business and Religion. This says a lot about who Ira is, as he has many interests and strives to do things with excellence.

Over his 25-year career to date, Ira has worked in the restaurant, e-commerce, print, and marketing industries. Most of Ira's career has been spent in a sales role in the print and graphics industry helping small and medium-sized businesses gain market share and increase sales. Since June 2020, with the launch of his company, Bowman Digital Media, Ira has focused on helping increase visibility for his clients on social media and increasing website traffic. The internet has become the primary source of commerce, and visibility is important to increase sales.

JOEL PHILLIPS

Tip 1: Make money first and fast

When you are starting a business, whether bootstrapped or well-funded, more often than not, you have a pool of resources you will use to begin operations, finalize a saleable product or service, start your sales process, and prepare to open the doors.

Most business owners start with the mindset that they have a specific amount of resources and runway available until those resources run out. By then, in their thinking, they will have a revenue stream that will overtake the money spent every month to keep the business running.

I have seen it time after time and this is exactly the wrong way to get your business started and off the ground. How do I know? Because this thinking nearly put me out of business. If this is the wrong approach, then what is the right approach?

The best way to start a business today is with no money—no funding, no friends and family, no equity share, and no outside resources. Even if you get money to operate until you get going, you need to function without it. You may ask, "Well, this is what the money is for—to operate, so why would I operate without it?"

For the most part, it is unrealistic to think you can start a business with no money, but the mindset is critical here.

No matter how well-funded you are, you must operate as if every dollar you spend is your last.

Why? Two primary reasons. When you operate this way, you don't dip into your money in the bank. Keep this on hand for emergencies and do everything you can not to touch it. Aside from helping you preserve capital, working this way has a far more significant impact on your employees and profitability.

When there is no cushion, the mindset and culture you generate are: "We need to make money now because if we don't, there *is* no tomorrow." When everyone is firing on all cylinders out of necessity, the difference in what they can accomplish is incredible. When you take off the training wheels, you will generate positive revenue far faster and may be amazed at what your employees can achieve.

Tip 2: Your digital footprint matters more than you know

According to a popular study, 81% of people research a business online before making a purchase decision. Nearly 76% of the population (according to the same study) does some percentage of shopping online. By the end of 2022, spending was projected to hit $5.5 trillion, with the numbers only increasing. Yet, here is a scary fact. Nearly 30% of small businesses still don't have a simple website.

Factor into this equation that most websites are subpar, with no customer journey, no online store, and no customer interaction. Add to that the fact that many CMS (content management systems) steal customer traffic while the top CMS in the world, with more than 40% of the website business, is by far the most vulnerable from a security perspective and the worst performing on mobile devices, a factor in Google ranking using Core Web Vitals. So, while we have studies that quote statistics about the number of small businesses that don't have a website, we can only guess that 70% of the small businesses that do have a website (the numbers are all over the board) have more than a static, poorly performing website that accomplishes nothing online.

Here is the kicker. Most people consider the website their digital footprint, but that isn't the case. Your digital footprint includes your entire online presence, including social media, videos, website, blogs, press releases, and anything else you can find about a company online. When you include all of these other facets of digital identity, most small businesses get overwhelmed and just shut down, giving up on the one thing that can amplify their traffic significantly with just a bit of attention.

Here is the tip, don't try to boil the ocean. Boiling the ocean is expensive and often ends up with zero results. Work with someone who knows what they are doing and who can help you take one small step at a time. Start with your website. It is more than just a calling card, so have it professionally designed. While much more expensive than doing it yourself, you are in business, and you need to let experts help you achieve an effective digital footprint with an engaging online presence that draws in clients and gets them through the sales funnels you and your expert develop.

Tip 3: Learn how to stay up on tech trends

This sounds way easier than it is. With technology changing significantly every five minutes, how do you stay up to date with the latest trends and products in a decidedly unforgiving and relentless space given how time-consuming any learning curve associated with technology is? You have a business to run. You rely on technology to help you run your business, but how do you build a stable foundation on shifting sands?

First of all, quit chasing the rabbit. You will never catch it. Instead of going around in circles you need to head in a straight line. Keeping up with technology is a mirage when it comes to solving the problems you have in your business. This doesn't mean it is a lost cause; it just means you must find ways to decrease the learning curve and stabilize your technological foundation.

How do you decrease the learning curve? There are several ways to accomplish this, but the best way is to hire a fractional CTO if you can afford to. If hiring a full-time or fractional CTO isn't in your budget, the next best choice is to find a technology partner that acts as your CTO from an advisory perspective. We found that this model is most effective when dealing with small businesses who don't have the resources to hire a fractional CTO but need the expertise to avoid all the landmines in the tech world. They can help you answer questions such as, *How do I avoid getting trapped in website or ecommerce platforms? What CRM do I need that can grow with me, and I can understand it without having to take certification courses? What should I be spend my money on?*

These are only a few of the valid questions, but the good news is that you are not alone. If not Proshark, then find a company willing to be your technical advisor and let them guide you through endless and expensive solutions. Then, when you are big enough, they or someone else can become your fractional CTO. If done correctly, you will be headed in the right direction, and technology will amplify your company voice rather than be the albatross around your neck.

Lesson Learned: Companies run out of money because of a culture of ambivalence toward revenue

As a new entrepreneur getting ready to launch your new business, you have tried to cover every angle to ensure you don't end up as just another statistic in the failed column. You have given every consideration and listened to the advice from every "smart" person you know and even some you don't know. You believe in your product or service and are willing to roll the dice because there is something better about how you do it that makes you think you can capture market share. You believe, and it shouldn't be any other way.

You completed your exhaustive competitive analysis and saw that the market does have competing companies, but there is room for your company, and you anticipate growth in your segment. Also, having competitors means there is a demand for what you will be selling. Otherwise, they would not exist.

More importantly, you have not made the age-old mistake of confusing market capacity as a way to capture market share. This means that you are solving a problem with your solution, and since you are solving a problem, you thoughtfully justify your ability to capture some market share. It sounds like you are on the right track so far.

Finally, you have talked to your friends and family, or maybe professional colleagues, who believe in what you want to do or build, so they will back you financially. Perhaps you are going the SBA or debt route to get funding for your project. Fantastic! We said it in the tips section, but here it is again. Most businesses don't fail because they are under-funded. That seems counter-intuitive, so how do we justify a statement like that?

It's pretty simple, really. Companies don't run out of money because they didn't ask for enough; they run out because of the culture of ambivalence toward revenue. In other words, a company could have double the funding they need but run out because the entire company has been trained not to focus on bringing in income.

Let me tell you a story about Proshark. When starting as a software development agency, we had a plan and a goal to get funded, build our platform, and become a major player in the SaaS (software as a service) space. Our product offering was good, and we developed a solid business plan.

Obtaining funding was not an issue as we had the basis for a competitive product that solved a problem in our proposed space. The mission and vision we created were clear, so investors could get onboard and had no problem backing our play. In fact, on paper, Proshark looked great. We checked all the boxes to become a success, or so we thought. If you haven't yet, as an entrepreneur, you will find that plans and reality rarely intersect.

The day came when we opened the doors, hired developers and admin staff, rolled up our sleeves, and got to work. We were humming along nicely without a care in the world as we burned through cash, working to get our platform up and running. Our focus never wavered, and we stayed heads-down in developing our platform called "mPro." As for burning our cash, it was okay in everybody's eyes because this was our runway (Cash On Hand divided by Burn Rate Per Month equals Total Time Before We Starve). Our projections were extremely conservative, and we even set a percentage aside in anticipation of our spending exceeding our bank account, thus extending the runway even further.

The backup plan was that we would sell digital marketing services as a way to soften the landing when it came time to stand on our own two feet. Coupled with projected platform subscriptions from a planned launch in Q4 22, it seemed reasonable that we would generate enough revenue to cover operating costs, repay debt, and put some cash aside every month to build our war chest. We were wrong.

We did not know then that most companies don't fail from lack of funding; they fail from lack of appropriate culture. You see, we fell into the same trap. Our goal was to build this great big thing but to make sure we launched the MVP (minimum viable product) in a lean fashion, use the feedback, and build as we go. The theory was to generate income as quickly as possible with revenue projections pre-baked into our burn. It was the worst philosophy of all time and nearly cost us the company.

The problem? Even though we focused on launching an MVP, our platform was a huge, and we tried to solve too many problems simultaneously. The idea was still good, and the execution was according to plan, but once again, plans do not always intersect with reality.

Our build was taking way too long, and even though we had beta clients on the platform, we could not get a release version we were comfortable with, and the development dragged on. Q4 22 came and went, and we still held beta on our platform. Digital marketing alone was not enough to carry us, so what would we do now? How did we end up in this position after carefully planning and working so hard to stick to the schedule?

Where did we go wrong? Revenue projections? Actual time to develop? Time to market? Estimated marketing spend? Labor costs? Runway estimations? Capital requirements using our existing model? The answer was yes to all of the above, but the real question was not "where" did we go wrong but "when" did we go wrong? The answer to that question was simple but elusive. I can't even take credit for the correct response, but it is one I will not deviate from in the future, no matter who I advise.

What is the answer? No need to hold your breath because here it is. "When" we went wrong is from the first day we decided to go into business – before we performed our first business function. Inadvertently, it was the culture we created and promoted as we opened the doors and started operations. The message we put out to our staff was that we had a planned period where we did not need to focus on making money, only on creating our platform. This planned period was communicated to all our employees and baked into every aspect of our operations.

We unintentionally crafted a culture with zero sense of urgency and zero sense of the need to be a revenue-generating company. Our culture became a relaxed stroll in the general direction of becoming another statistic. The worst part was that the inevitable wasn't apparent to us as we inched forward. We didn't have a clue until it was almost too late.

Also, it should be no surprise that, as we constantly kept moving toward the end of our runway, nobody had any urgency surrounding the blatant fact that we were way behind on our revenue projections. Digital marketing was not enough to pick up the slack. Was it too late? No matter how urgent we, as upper management, made the problem, the company's culture was set, and correcting our course became a monumental task. How do you retrain an entire company to change its attitude from entitlement to survival in a short period? That is a story for another book.

It is easy to comprehend how, by the time most companies realize the problem, it is too late, and they have no option other than to generate more runway by borrowing more to try to solve the problem. It isn't easy because the sharks know when a company is desperate and are far less likely to give any favorable terms to companies in dire straits. Ultimately, if you cannot generate more runway, you are out of business. This is where most companies fail, and this is our lesson learned.

We were fortunate. At Proshark, we were able to soften the landing with our digital marketing services just enough to allow us to impact our company culture, turn the ship before it hit the rocks, and develop additional revenue streams around web, mobile app, and automation development. Still, there was a period where it was touch and go.

After consulting and advising the boards and CEOs of many different companies and after serving roles in multiple C-Suite and fractional CTO and CEO positions, there is only one thing I will focus on when advising a company in crisis or a new company just getting started (and everything in between)—revenue first and revenue fast. There are multiple ways to get there, but that has to be the primary focus at any stage of the game.

As for Proshark, we are now 100% focused as a company on generating revenue with every activity we perform. We are deepening each of our service channels to provide standalone revenue streams with the idea that our survival depends on the performance of each channel.

For your company, out of the gate, create that sense of urgency where your employees know they must produce income to get paid next month. If they don't, they go hungry, or the business fails altogether. Even if you have money, you don't have money. When you sit back and rely for even a month on the money you have in the bank versus what you have coming in the door, you negatively impact your organization's culture. Managing your company culture can sometimes be more important than managing your company.

ABOUT THE AUTHOR

A seasoned entrepreneur, Joel is CEO and founder of Proshark as well as founder, CTO, and Global Managing Partner of the Strategic Advisor Board. He has extensive experience in leadership, innovation, software development, automation, app development, data sciences, analytics, cybersecurity, and real estate.

He serves on multiple boards and believes the next step in technological evolution brings the convergence of blockchain, artificial intelligence, augmented reality, and data sciences.

- Member of Mensa, Bellwether, and ACA

- Licensed Real Estate Broker with commercial development experience

- Resume includes 4G Development, Sony Pictures Digital Entertainment, eAssist Global Solutions, and American Loans

- Volunteer work includes J Ryley Foundation, Habitat for Humanity, and Planning Commission Chairman

- Hobbies include flying, sailing, golfing, biking, music, and music production

JANET HOGAN

Tip 1: Just because you can, doesn't mean you should

Dear reader, this is not just a tip. It's the hardest won lesson of my life. It's a lesson that's cost me thirty precious years and just as many millions of dollars. I share it with you now, so you might save yourself all that time and money.

Having a talent for something is not a good enough reason to turn it into an enterprise. If you start any business just because you can, I guarantee it will become a monster that will suck the life out of you and have you constantly asking, *"Why the hell did I get myself into this mess, and how do I get myself out?!"*

How do I know this?

1981. My husband was gifted with an extraordinary palate. Long story short, we set up a restaurant that was an instant hit, winning every food award, but which we sold out of just twelve months later, exhausted, battle weary, and on the brink of divorce.

1992. I have a talent for words and a degree in communications. I joined an ad agency, became the youngest writer in Australia to win a Lion at Cannes (adland's version of the Oscars), and decided that if my bosses could do it, so could I. Oddfellows Advertising quickly became the highest-profile boutique agency in our hometown of Sydney, Australia. Four years later, we sold out, exhausted, battle weary, and in need of a sea change.

1996. We moved to the Whitsundays, Down Under's answer to the Caribbean. My husband has a talent for landscaping, and there was a 120-acre block of waterfront land for sale.

"Let's turn it into Australia's first garden suburb."

Eleven years later, we sold the last block. Exhausted. Battle weary. But this time, with several million under our belt.

2008. The Great Recession. Thanks to a risky margin loan, the millions in the black became millions in the red. Okay. What if we turned our mansion by the sea into a wedding venue?

Because we could, we did. Again.

Fast forward seven years, our mansion by the sea morphed into an international company, turning over many millions, employing sixty people, and expanding to Bali, where again we picked up a bundle of awards.

We sold out three years later, exhausted, battle weary, and with no more appetite for risk.

Do you see the pattern?

Yes, we had talent, but we always ended up back where we started. Older, but not so much wiser.

Was Steve Jobs's talent for design enough to create the Apple phenomenon?

Was Richard Branson's knack for clever marketing all it took to launch and grow Virgin?

No.

Talent aside, you must add two other critical ingredients to your mix before you are ready to bake that pie called My Successful Business.

Tip 2: Let passion, not money, be your carrot

When I look back, the justification for starting up each of our businesses was always *"...and we could make good money doing this."*

The word "passion," a little like "purpose," was not in my lexicon. It was one of those words that kind of irritated me. I didn't want to be some kind of pontificating zealot; I just wanted to have the freedom to be my own boss. And make a decent living in the process.

Sound familiar?

This is where I am going to get preachy.

Without all-consuming passion, you will not persevere through the challenges that will ultimately beset you. Looking back, we mistook sacrificing ourselves on the altar of hard work as a noble trait. The truth is hard work without passion is ultimately life-zapping. And kind of pointless.

Why didn't I know this at the time?

I mindlessly followed in the footsteps of my father, the first ear surgeon in the world to implant a cochlear implant (bionic ear device) in an infant. And a chronic workaholic. Every night he would trudge through the front door saying: *"They got their pound of flesh today."*

We don't just inherit genetic traits like red hair and green eyes from our parents. We inherit their beliefs and behavior patterns too.

So how do you find something as nebulous as passion?

Well, it doesn't get much weirder than this.

By confronting your pain.

Which, twenty-five years, $70 million, and five businesses later, I finally did.

We all have our unique brand of pain.

Mine was the ickiest of all: the agonizingly slow death of self-betrayal that comes when you bury yourself alive under a ton of work.

I'd spent my whole life following the mantra: Work hard. Make money. Get happy.

What I now realized was it was not the elements that were wrong, but the order they were in.

If you aspire to be a more conscious entrepreneur, here's my heartfelt mantra for you:

Get happy and passionate about what you choose to do. Work hard, and the money will flow.

Now that I am finally making a living doing what I love, I see every penny that lands in my bank account as the universe clapping.

So where to from here?

Step 1: Find out what you feel you must do (your passion.) Clue: it almost invariably springs from your greatest source of pain, usually, but not always, as a child.

Like the entrepreneur whose brother was run over by a bus and rendered a paraplegic. The pain of that gave him the passion today to organize triathlons so that hundreds of thousands of people know the freedom of living fit and healthy lives.

Or the successful CEO of a major accountancy firm who experienced the pain of his father going bankrupt. Today he works with other business owners to ensure they don't end up the same.

Or the real estate developer who lived through the pain of losing his family home as a boy. His newfound passion is providing an affordable roof over the heads of people who would otherwise be homeless.

Sacrificing yourself for something your heart is not in is a recipe for misery. The universe will not applaud you; it will take the money away, or worse, leave you always wanting more.

Why settle for an occupation that is slowly killing you when you can have a *preoccupation* that brings you back to life?

Before you launch any new venture, take pen to paper and ask these three questions:

1. *What areas of my life have caused me the greatest pain?*

2. *How can I use that pain to fuel my passion and spare others that pain?*

3. *What I actually feel like doing is....*

Listen not to your doubting mind but to the source of your passion—your intuitive, courageous heart. Your heart goals are the real goals that will deliver you financial freedom and fulfillment.

Tip 3: Your business isn't about you; it's about the problem you are here to solve

Great businesses are not born from seizing an unexpected opportunity. Or the love of a quick buck. They stem from a genuine desire to solve a problem causing at least some level of frustration and, ideally, palpable pain.

What better example than the phenomenon of Covid, forcing billions of people into an extended state of lockdown, made ten times worse by the roll-on cost of financial loss, mental stress, and anxiety.

The vaccines for this new type of virus, predicted to be many years away, were developed in less than eighteen months.

The bigger the problem, the greater the value of the solution.

Other examples:

Problem: *I want to go on a holiday but can't find an affordable place to stay.*
Solution: Airbnb.

Problem: *The planet cannot afford petrol-guzzling cars.*
Solution: Tesla.

Problem: *No one in my organization knows what anybody else is doing.*
Solution: Slack.

Get the idea?

The bigger the problem, the more people will pay you to solve it for them.

So what are the three ingredients for a successful, long-term business?

1. Something you have a natural aptitude for. (Tip 1)

2. Something you care deeply about. (Tip 2)

3. The product of 1 and 2 combined applied to a real problem in the marketplace for which you can create a unique solution. (Tip 3)

The intersection of these three aspects is your business sweet spot, and once you have cracked it, you will be set to make a living you love.

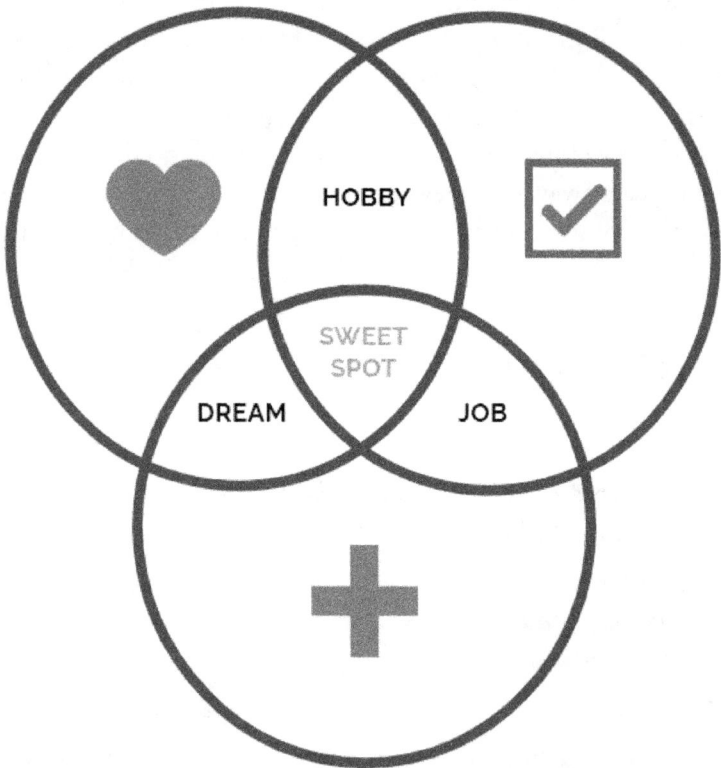

The biggest lesson I've learned?

Before you can successfully work *for* yourself, you must work *on* yourself.

Lesson Learned: If you want to grow your net worth, start with your self-worth

Did you ever play shops as a kid?

I remember going around our house looking for things to sell. A tin of baked beans from the pantry, a teething ring from my sister's playpen, nail clippers from the bathroom… I would carefully arrange my merchandise on our front steps and sell them to Nikki, my cherished teddy bear and first, never-complaining customer.

It wasn't that big a leap for me at fifteen to nail a sign up to our front gate:

> *"Janet's Pavlova Pantry. Filled pavlova: $14. Shell only: $7. Delivery included."*

The business flourished.

Until the day the whole family piled into my dad's tiny Toyota Avanza to deliver a major order. There were four of us balancing a pavlova on our laps and one in our hands on our way to a prestigious Historical Society luncheon. My dad, whose skills at microscopic inner ear surgery didn't extend to driving, hit the brakes a little too hard, converting the inside of his pristine car to a snowstorm of strawberries, cream, and meringue. That's when he turned to me and said, *"Janet, I think it's time to focus on your studies."*

But that wasn't enough to kill my love of trading. Today, the Malvern Star bicycle and ten-foot fiberglass dinghy I bought from the proceeds of my pavlova business are still two of my most treasured possessions.

It planted in me this idea that a successful business was as simple as providing a product or service in exchange for money.

I was yet to learn that one vital ingredient was missing from that formula. A lesson that would take me four businesses and forty years of hard slog to discover.

Up until that discovery, you would frequently hear me lament:

How come I'm grinding away 24/7, carrying all the stress of meeting payroll, when all I've done is given myself a salary, and not even a regular one at that?

Whether it was creating advertising campaigns for everything from breakfast cereal to pantyhose, selling blocks of land to sea changers, or wedding packages to couples tying the knot in Bali, we would make loads of money. And burn through it just as quickly.

So what, you may be wondering, was I missing?

Financial education? Discipline? A proper business plan? Yes.

But even more important than those was the one critical piece if we are to come away with any sense of personal success and fulfillment at the end of this complex maze called life.

The one thing our upbringing, education system, or social programming seems to place no value on.

The one thing I was blissfully unaware of.

Self-mastery.

I had no idea who I was, let alone what I was supposed to do with my life.

I'd just put my head down and followed the mantra of *"The harder I work, the more money I make, and the happier I'll be"* until I finally did get everything I thought I wanted. A waterfront mansion by the sea in a tropical paradise that would have been the envy of Richard Branson. Plus, a solid marriage, three beautiful daughters, and money in the bank.

But I'll never forget the day I was in the kayak with my daughter Clover, surveying everything we owned.

Instead of the promised happiness, all I felt was emptiness.

The thought of confronting that inner void filled me with fear. Would I be opening a Pandora's box of dark truths that would plunge me into an even deeper hole?

So I did nothing.

And because I didn't take action, the universe took it for me.

Throwing me the curve ball that was the 2008 Great Recession. As our thirty years of hard-earned wealth went down the gurgler, I went with it.

I will never forget my dark night of the soul, wheeling around our garden at two in the morning, feeling the nauseous shame of taking out a risky margin loan, and in the process, destroying everything we'd worked so hard for till I finally concluded that the world would be a better place without me.

I believe there are two kinds of death. Physical, where we take our own life and leave all our suffering behind for our loved ones to deal with. Or metaphysical, where we have to let something inside of us die for the true self to emerge.

I had to let go of this belief that business success was all about sacrificing myself on the altar of hard work.

The time had come, I realized, to finally confront that thing I had spent my whole life avoiding.

Me.

I engaged a therapist and moved our family to the personal development epicenter of the world, Bali, where I signed up for almost every inner-work program in my inbox.

However, after investing ten years and tens of thousands of dollars, I came to a disturbing realization. I had a sackful of insights but nothing that felt like a permanent change. Even worse, no one seemed too phased by that. There was no accountability, no follow-up.

I decided to go cold turkey on workshops and channel my frustration into something more productive.

Advertising has taught me two precious lessons.

1. For every problem, there is a solution.

2. If you accept someone's money, you must deliver a real, tangible outcome in return.

And so I decided to create the program I wish someone had taken me through when I was at the bottom of my dark pit.

Following Steven Covey's *7 Habits of Highly Effective People*, I applied his Habit Number 2: Begin with the End in Mind.

To create my program, I worked backward from the result I wanted.

What was the holy grail I was seeking?

More than money, I wanted something more profound, more satisfying. Financial reward plus a feeling of deep fulfillment. I narrowed it down to one word.

Prosperity.

But before I could enjoy physical and emotional wealth, I would need a reason to get out of bed every morning, something bigger than myself to keep pulling me forward.

A sense of purpose.

Until now, I had never truly believed I had much value. Now, I know we all have a gift or unique brand of genius. Before I could achieve my purpose, I would first need to understand my gift. Only then could I step into my true power. This became the next goal.

Power.

Before I could understand my true power, I would first have to unlock that unique energy that is the source of our motivation. That great force that had till now remained a mystery to me.

Passion.

And before I could feel that passion, I would first need to confront the one thing I'd spent my whole life avoiding.

The one thing we all share a deep fear of being overwhelmed by.

That connects us to others through empathy.

That if you embrace and follow it will guide you to prosperity.

And yes, it's another P word.

Probably the most important one of all.

Pain.

Of all the parts that make us human, mental or emotional pain is what we've been programmed to see as bad. Our default strategy is all too often to go into denial or pop a pill and numb it.

And yet, our pain, that deeply rooted, suppressed yearning of the soul, is our golden key to success.

All you need is the courage to confront, understand and ultimately allow it to guide you.

So what was my pain?

Perhaps the deepest pain of all.

Self-betrayal.

By following the carrot of money and endless, blind achievement, I'd buried myself alive until I had no idea who the real me truly was.

The only way to end this self-betrayal was to follow the path of its opposite: self-mastery. I had to bring this pain to light, unleash my passion, step into my power, find my purpose and create a world of prosperity for myself and others.

Today, five years later, that is precisely what I'm doing through The 5th Door, the program designed to help frustrated entrepreneurs transition from pain to prosperity.

After forty years of living as the guru of what not to do, I joined the likes of HuffPost founder Arianna Huffington, Coca-Cola inventor John Stith Pemberton, and McDonald's Ray Kroc, who likewise found their true success after age fifty, when most other entrepreneurs are thinking of retiring.

But why would I ever want to retire? I've finally found the secret to making a living I love, which is what I'm not teaching my fellow entrepreneurs and business owners.

So this, my friends, is the one big lesson that reset the course of my life, and I hope it does the same for you.

The hard part is not making the money. It's becoming the person who is big enough to hold onto that money, to love it, grow it, and use it to change not only your life but the lives of many others for the better so you, too, discover what it means to live a happy and prosperous life.

ABOUT THE AUTHOR

Janet proudly calls herself "the guru of what not to do" despite spending forty years heading up four businesses turning over $70 million in industries as diverse as hospitality, advertising, real estate development, and even destination wedding management.

If anyone knows what it is to ride the rollercoaster of business triumph and tragedy, it's this veteran of enterprise from Down Under.

Today she is the very successful, and more importantly, happy and fulfilled Founder and CEO of The 5th Door, the breakthrough program she created to help established and aspiring business owners cross the threshold of radical self-awareness so they can make a living doing what they love, without having to take all the tumbles she took to get there.

DR. ANDREA RENEE RIVERA, DACM, LAC.

I dedicate this chapter and my life thus forward to honoring my mother, who died on March 25, 2023. May the life she gave me and all the sacrifices she and my father made personally on my behalf be justified by the value my life contributes to humanity. I am forever grateful to God, my family, real friends, teachers, and colleagues, without whom I would have already died and would have nothing of value internally or externally to stand on or contribute.

Tip 1: Marketing: *You* are your customer

"I once was blind, but now I see."

—John Newton, "Amazing Grace"

Many business owners need help to define their mission statement, purpose, business plan, and ideal customer avatar they created their business to serve. I spent hundreds of hours over nine years, from 2010 to 2019, and over $27,000 in marketing business training seminars trying to get clear on how to define who my customer was, what their pain points were, and what services I could offer to help my ideal customer solve their problems.

Finally, over the past four years, I realized that confusion comes from looking outside of yourself in the marketplace for a general customer service opportunity rather than searching deep within to discover the self-evident answer revealed in our life experiences. Clarity came from doing my 2019 website brand story video with the insightful, master communicator and LA filmmaker Evan Galeano. I realized that we all have a cause for which our specific life experience sets us up to be the spokesperson. Evan asked me what problems I had faced and solved in my life. My life review revealed the self-evident service and customer that my life calls me to contribute to humanity. Our businesses can help people like us walk through those same problems we have overcome.

You are your customer. Do what you know and speak honestly from your heart and real-life experience. Look to serve who you used to be. Be for others what you needed and didn't have. Be an authentic example of walking your talk and doing what is organic and engaging. Your customer will feel you understand them and their needs. They will feel safe and trust you because they know you have been in their shoes and have encountered similar problems. You are an example of what is possible with the practical map they need to get the results you achieved. You offer the services you didn't have when you needed them the most. You help the person you used to be to avoid the land mines you stepped on and take advantage of the opportunities you missed so they enjoy a less rocky, painful, and delayed road to their vision of success.

Tip 2: Sales: Research your market and use the keystone pricing model to guarantee profits

"Profitability isn't an event; it's a habit."
—Mike Michalowicz, *Profit First: Transform Your Business from a Cash-Eating Monster to a Money-Making Machine*

Review your local ZIP Code census and analyze your successful competitors to know what your market wants and will pay for your services. Using this data, price your products and services using the keystone price rule that will guarantee you always make a profit. The keystone is wholesale price double the cost of the product's manufacture or service delivery, and the retail price is double the wholesale price. With this keystone model for your pricing, profits can occur from start-up and continue during growth. Between the wholesale and retail prices, you have room for necessary affiliate partners' commissions, sales reps' commissions, and markdown incentives for customer loyalty and motivated action. You guarantee you are always doubling or quadrupling your investment of time and money in any sale and keeping the cost of doing business at 25% of the retail prices of your products and services. This will guarantee adequate profits, long-term financial stability, and business sustainability.

Use these top ten strategies to keep your cost of delivering your services down and your profit margin at two to four times your hard prices of human capital, time, and money.

1. Use college interns for free and discounted labor to cut your costs of administrative management, marketing, manufacturing, and delivery of your business services to your customer.

2. Outsource administrative labor overseas with VAs to cut the cost of employee salaries.

3. Use 1099 independent contractors instead of W2 employees.

4. Use technology to leverage your working hours and create passive streams of income.

    a. Automate administrative tasks
    b. Create evergreen prerecorded media-based products

    c. Create group programs and services that maximize your hourly labor income beyond a limited one-on-one service-based model

5. Consider being a manufacturer of products and services using raw materials or intellectual property you create to cut the cost of materials, tools, and talent necessary to make your product or service. Don't buy wholesale products from another company to sell retail.

6. Share office space, resources, subscriptions for professional services, etc., to reduce business overhead costs.

7. Delegate and work with a team that fills in your competency gaps. Use Dr. Andrea's 5 Element Archetype evaluation to discover your and your team's personality type, strengths, and self-management style that identifies what you and your customers need and what support your team needs to thrive.

8. As a start-up, you can wear many hats in your business. Don't wear all hats in one single day. It is exhausting and takes you out of a zone of quality, efficiency, and productivity reached within one to two hours of doing a task. Cycling through many hats reduces the quality of the work and limits results.

9. Remember that having a team and taking the time to reflect on milestones and challenges creates the essential magnification of the powerful emotional energy and the community support needed to keep going.

10. Build referral relationships. See Tip 3, Ending Island Syndrome, to explore partnering with colleagues to pool resources and clients to reduce costs and increase client base and sales.

Tip 3: Disrupting your market: End Island Syndrome

"A team is not a group of people who work together.
A team is a group of people who trust each other."

—Simon Sinek, *Together is Better*

End the self-defeating and limiting Island Syndrome of working as a lone wolf from a fear-based perspective looking at others as threatening competition. There is no competition. There is no zero-sum game to play in life or business. No one can do life alone. Always seek win/win partnerships. Share customers. Refer your customers to great products and services. Offer complimentary services to the same customers of your referral partners and be flooded with referrals. Seek to join forces and serve all involved. Stop thinking there are not enough customers, and you are competing for them. No one is you, and there is no competition when you are being your unique self and contributing uniquely. Your customers and referral partners relate to you, want to work with you specifically, and want to be loyal to you.

The purpose of relationships is to magnify emotion. E-motion is energy facilitating motion. Manifestation comes from the e-motion we cultivate. A passionate, enthusiastic, and confident person attracts. You cannot attract success with a fear-based lack mentality that is critical and combative. The e-motion you feel most often and boldly attracts or repels the people and opportunities that move or stall success in every area of life. We can't make enough e-motion alone. We inevitably become limited by our isolated narrow view and experience, overwhelmed, exhausted, and finally burned out. Be a vibrant team player and share the wins.

Lesson Learned: Clarity is king: Know yourself and the game of business

"We must realize that the cause underlying most failures to effectual prayer is muddled thinking and lack of emotional control."

—Dr. Joseph Murphy, *The Wheels of Truth*

Businesses start and thrive or die based on their owner's personal awareness, mindset, vision of what is possible, and examples they follow that are set by their chosen circle of influence. The owner's perception of their business experience drives their emotions and behavior, creating success and failure. Being nineteen and a naïve, ignorant, poor, college student from a five-figure working-class family, I was unprepared to keep seven-figure success in the NYC fashion accessory industry. I didn't know I needed mentors or models of success to follow. I didn't see the game of business, the rules, myself, or the players.

Falling miserably back down into poverty within four years post-9/11 was heartbreaking. Personal and financial recovery took me fourteen years. Surviving the COVID-19 pandemic lockdowns as an essential front-line physician in CA took me back to the edge of poverty again. The biggest lesson I can offer from my experience of two trips to business heaven and hell and back again is to invite you to dedicate time to finding out what you don't know. You can get clear by sincerely answering, at least once a year, these five essential big-picture questions that can clarify your vision, core values, strategy, and quality of life experience:

1. Why am I doing my work? Is my heart in it? Does it feed my spirit?

2. What value does the work I am doing contribute to society? Is it worth living and dying for to me?

3. What is my definition of success, and how is it based explicitly upon my core values, and am I living it?

4. Who are past and currently living examples of people that were/are living my core value-based successful life I want that I can model? If they are alive, how could I collaborate with them?

5. Where can I get mentorship support, direction, and insight from someone who has achieved what I want to help me understand the game of business and life, refine my vision of success, and teach me the fundamental tools and strategy for sustainability and quality of life success? The Small Business Administration's Small Business Development Centers offer mentorship for free.

For the past sixteen years, I have found it essential to keep asking these big questions. I did not ask these questions in 1992 when I started my first jewelry design, manufacture, and sales business at nineteen. I just saw the opportunity to go to an NYC street fair market, pay $50 for a table to sell jewelry, and earn the money I desperately needed to buy a winter coat and eat. It took me four years working in my business to start thinking about these big questions for the first time. But I didn't start seriously attempting to answer these big questions clearly and deeply within myself until 2007. My health, business, marriage, and whole life, in general, were utterly obliterated over the four years following the post-9/11 economic hardships that led me to a two-year health crisis, followed by bankruptcy and divorce from my business partner and dissolution of my business I had for thirteen years.

I learned that hard work is not always the answer to every need and problem and can cause many issues to fester unnoticed and unattended. I was too busy to think about what I was doing and its long-term impact on my life and business. I was not working smart. I was mindlessly immersed in the "just do it" Nike-coined, slogan-driven society where taking action is king, material successes are pursued and celebrated the loudest, and work is made the primary focus of our lives at the expense of everything else. All my peers were doing the same. My big life decisions, like how to live, where to live, the type of career path to choose, and the people I decided to be in professional relationships with were based on the opportunities for more growth and the material wealth they would offer. I didn't have a clear, core, value-based success model vision as the north star for my business or life. I didn't have a strategic map to navigate and follow.

When making primarily growth and money-based decisions, I unconsciously sacrificed my integrity, making choices that compromised my health, wealth, relationships, and quality of my work. When I felt the pain of these personal sacrifices, I attempted to justify them under the illusion that the growth opportunities and material wealth results would make the sacrifices worth it. Sadly, these choices did not necessarily lead to the bigger material wealth payoff "success" due to the ever-increasing costs of doing business that the growth required.

A book on that subject, *Profit First*, explains how companies can fall into the trap of development that results in ever-decreasing profits. Having an ever-bigger circus to manage also reduced my awareness and bandwidth for the vitally necessary insightful evaluation of what and how I was working, whom I was working with and for, and the tangible results. I was wearing too many hats and managing too many moving parts beyond my ability. As an overworked and overextended solopreneur, I slowly woke up to realize, mainly through crisis events, that I was working with people who didn't share my ethics and core values, let alone my vision and definition of success.

Furthermore, from getting caught up in the emotionally reactive, defensive action-based crisis management of the circus I unwittingly self-created, I also got disconnected from my work's meaningful and fulfilling aspects. With little time and energy for myself or personal relationships, I also didn't develop the community and mentorship relationships that could have helped me stop and ask the big questions and see the truth of the results of what I was doing and how to transform what I was doing into a better healthier, happier, and more fulfilling way of life and working.

I fell into the quicksand of earning money first, which was easy to do since I was physically hungry and struggling to meet basic survival needs when I started my business. As a scholarship kid in NYC without enough money to eat properly, I was highly motivated to start my own business in my "spare" time around full-time school and two part-time jobs. And I was highly motivated to overwork at any level required to make my business grow as a means of climbing out of poverty. My life was a recipe for disaster, creating unsustainable work habits and lifestyles at the expense of my health and personal relationships that were inevitably self-imploding.

I bought into defining success by growth and being busy. I did not think about the quality of character of whom I was working with or the quality of life I would have around work. I did not know how the long hours would affect my health or relationships with my business partner, husband, friends, or family. I worked eighty to one hundred hours a week for four years without a vacation to reach the goal of buying my own home. I didn't see my family for holidays for most of the thirteen years I had my business. I did not take an entire day off, even once a week. I was living for my business to grow and make more money to survive and then later thrive, growing materially. I thought the American dream was owning a home and being busy at work at any cost. I was naïve and didn't realize how harmful this was.

I don't recommend doing life and business as I did with my first jewelry business. It almost killed me, and it destroyed my finances, marriage, and business. I offer my experience as an cautionary tale to help you make far wiser and better-informed decisions than I knew how to make. Ideally, now, with this book, you can avoid the pitfalls, significant losses, and suffering-packed roller coaster ride I fell into over the last thirty-one years. I intend to contribute my experiences to this book and help you become an aware, conscious, intentional, and whole person and avoid my sixteen-year rise and crash and thirty-one-year uphill resiliency journey. You can be resilient, living your definition of success now. You can do better than I did with less suffering. I'm dedicated to helping you do that for your benefit and your life's contribution to humanity.

ABOUT THE AUTHOR

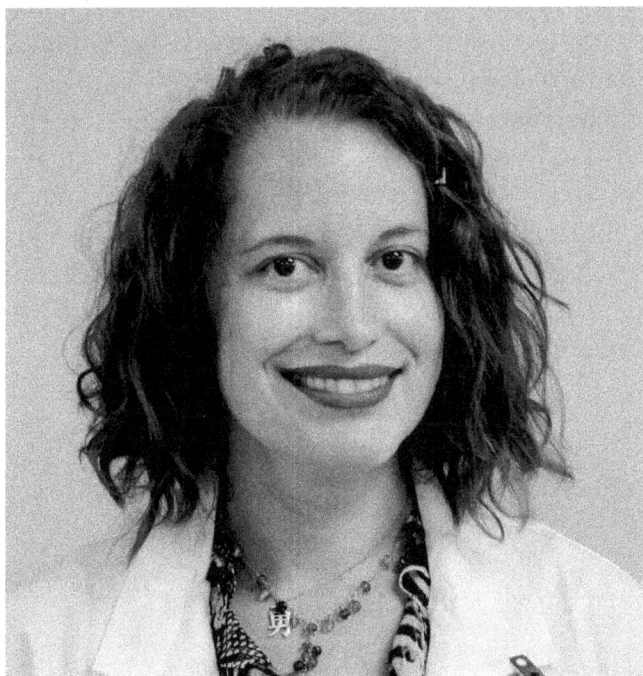

From 1992 to 2007, Dr. Andrea Renee, DACM, LAc. enjoyed fifteen years of international acclaim as the president and founder of Andrea Renee, Inc., an innovative jewelry design and manufacturing house based in SOHO NYC. Her collection was carried in the top global department stores, including Barney's NY & Japan, Daimaru Japan, Fortunoff, Bloomingdales, Macy's, and Nordstrom, as well as her own

SOHO NYC boutique with celebrity clients including Drew Barrymore, Johnny Depp, and Julianne Moore. She enjoyed recognition as one of New York Magazine's "favorite downtown jewelry designers." Andrea was featured as her company spokesperson in media coverage, including *NY Times, NY Magazine, In Style, Entertainment Weekly, Seventeen, Elle, Cosmo & Savvy Japan, NY Post, Time Out,* and *Good Day NY.*

Since 2007, she has delivered over 9,000 coaching and treatment sessions as a peak performance healthy lifestyle coach and Doctor of Acupuncture and Chinese Medicine. She is a certified yoga instructor and meditation teacher and has taught exercise therapy since 2007. Also, getting certified in 2011 as a Passion Test for Life and Business coach, Andrea coaches small business owners. As a licensed Acupuncturist primary care physician in CA, she is extensively trained in both Eastern and Western integrative, functional, and preventative medicine as well as nutrition, pain management/orthopedics, acupressure massage, energy work, and herbal medicine.

TONIA STONEY

Tip 1: Run your business like your ministry

Embracing your true self in business

Successful business owners understand that running a business goes beyond financial success. They know how crucial it is to treat customers, teammates, and partners with integrity and respect. By running your business like a ministry, you can lay a strong foundation of values that guides you through the ups and downs of entrepreneurship.

Identifying your fundamental core values is vital to managing your business like it's your ministry. Just as a church has guiding principles, a company should have a set of core values that reflect its beliefs and principles. Think like a customer for a moment. How would you like to be treated? You expect to be treated with respect, honesty, fairness, and professionalism when you or your child go to a store or educational setting, in person or online. You or your child deserve this.

I'll never forget how, when I was young and impressionable, my piano teacher told me what I could never do. She said I'd never be good enough to play classical or gospel music in church. As a kid, I honestly looked up to and admired my piano instructor as a role model. It's unbelievable the things you never forget. I remember that day clearly and am grateful

I chose not to let her comments determine my destiny. After she said those words to me, I promised myself that day to never talk negatively to children when I became an adult. Instead, I would only speak life and positivity into their lives, and I still do this today.

Running your business like a ministry, based on the Golden Rule, makes customers feel appreciated and respected, and they are more willing to promote your brand. They will promote your products and services and become brand ambassadors. This form of organic promotion (free promotion) is priceless and can have a massive impact on your company's growth and success.

Authenticity is a powerful tool for business. In a world where people want genuine relationships, being true to yourself and your business is essential. When you're open and honest about who you are, you form deeper bonds with your clients and team. People are drawn to companies with unique voices and authentic stories to tell.

One of new business owners' most significant mistakes is trying to be something they're not. I did this for a while and kept hitting a brick wall. Do you know that feeling of being a hamster who can't escape its wheel? That was me until I told myself, *Screw this! I'm just going to be myself. I was led to start this company, and from now on, I won't be comparing myself to anyone but the person God made me to be.*

Copying successful organizations' techniques or brand identities is easy, but it usually dilutes the message and lacks authenticity. Instead, embrace your true self and allow it to shine through in every part of your company, from the goods or services you offer to how you market them. Celebrate what makes you unique. Customers will gravitate toward your honest and authentic approach.

Tip 2: Go from distraction to focus

The power of now

You have started a fantastic adventure as a brand-new business owner, one that is full of limitless opportunities and exciting challenges. You're determined to make your mark and create something truly remarkable. And when trying to be successful, it's easy to let endless demands and distractions get in the way.

I used to be lost in the unending demands and distractions. After a few short years in business, my family criticized me for working nonstop. A valuable lesson I learned about the power of being present now guides my entrepreneurial journey. I didn't realize how much I worked until my nine-year-old niece labeled me a "workaholic."

Let me ask you a question. Do you often find yourself caught in a vortex of multitasking, juggling multiple responsibilities, and continuously dividing your attention? We have mastered the art of being physically present while mentally absent. Our bodies are at home with our families, but our minds are preoccupied with work. In contrast, at work, our thoughts drift to personal matters. This constant multitasking limits our productivity and ability to genuinely connect with others and make a difference in every aspect of our lives.

So, my dear friend, I challenge you to embrace the challenge of being in the now. When you're with your family, be there wholeheartedly. Give them your complete attention. Engage in meaningful conversations, make beautiful memories, and appreciate priceless moments. The work will always be there, but your loved ones deserve your complete presence and love.

Similarly, consciously choose to be fully immersed in your tasks and responsibilities at work. Refrain from being interrupted and distracted. Be deliberate with your time and energy. Focus on the job at hand and put your heart into it.

By giving your full attention to your work, you'll get great results and inspire those around you.

I recognize it's easier said than done, especially when work and personal obligations are overwhelming. Let me share a few practical strategies that have helped me along the way.

- **Set boundaries:** Dedicate time to work, family, self-care, and relaxation. Yes, I schedule these times on my calendar. Communicate these boundaries with your loved ones and team. Create a structure that lets you be present in all areas of your life.

- **Practice mindfulness**: Develop the habit of being fully present and aware of the moment. Stop, relax, and pay attention to your surroundings every day. By training your mind to be in the moment, you'll be able to pay more attention to the job at hand and enjoy life's pleasures.

- **Remember the bigger picture:** Building a successful business is not just about financial gains—it's about creating a meaningful life. It means giving your full attention and interest to whatever is happening right now. By mastering the art of being present, you unlock the capacity to connect deeply with your loved ones, excel at your work, and lead your business to greatness.

Tip 3: Invest in yourself

The power of professional development and building intentional relationships

Know the value of investing in yourself through professional development and building intentional relationships as you begin your business journey. These factors can potentially shape your business's trajectory while fueling your personal growth. When you invest in yourself, you are fostering your personal growth and development and improving your business-related skills and knowledge.

I thought professional development meant taking courses, joining professional organizations, and attending conferences. Imagine this: The world has shut down, and no one can leave their homes. Your entrepreneurial world has paused during your most successful year ever. Your services are only available in person, which means no one can use them. What happens now?

That was me.

At this point, I understood the power of my investments. I learned that intentional connections and professional development go hand in hand. One of my scariest entrepreneurial moments was the COVID-19 lockdown. How could I continue to teach kids who came to my house for lessons? No one knew how long the closure would last, and I was determined not to let it disrupt my business. I was overjoyed that my professional peers felt the same way. Within 48 hours, the piano community collaborated via social media groups to move our specialized group lessons online. *This* is the power of intentional relationships.

But the wonders of intentional relationships did not stop there. These business connections turned into friendships that will last a lifetime. I established deep and meaningful bonds with people I had never even met in person. The power of these friendships transformed my entrepreneurial journey, bringing support, inspiration, and a sense of camaraderie that extended far beyond the business realm.

Let my story remind you never to underestimate the value of investing in yourself. Professional development and intentional relationship building serve as bridges that lead to collaboration, support, and countless opportunities. I strongly encourage you to seek out mentors, industry experts, and other entrepreneurs who share your vision and values. Through deliberate partnerships, you will find direction, wisdom, and a sense of belonging in the entrepreneurial community.

Allow the power of self-investment and intentional relationship-building to catapult you to greatness!

Daring to succeed: Launching your business beyond fear and self-doubt

A piano teacher's perspective

A wave of anxiety washed over me as I stood in a room filled with music educators at an exclusive conference. An overwhelming sense of unworthiness and doubt engulfed me. This was my first music teacher conference as an entrepreneur, and the room was flooded with educators with far more teaching experience than I had. I lacked the impressive credentials and professional degrees in music that some of my colleagues possessed. They were respected authorities in their profession who had earned PhDs and trained at prestigious conservatories. I couldn't help but feel like a fraud as self-doubt seeped into my mind. I questioned my qualifications and wondered if I truly belonged there. In comparison, I felt like a speck in the universe.

In retrospect, I wish I had known what I know now. It's normal to feel a range of emotions when starting a business, including the dread of failure, fear of the unknown, and fear of being exposed as a fraud. These emotions can be excruciatingly paralyzing, leading you to question your skills and the goals and dreams you have set for yourself. However, I want to reassure you, my friend, that you are not traveling through this experience alone.

I want to take a moment to be transparent and vulnerable with you. This is the story of my personal experience as a business owner. I hope it will provide encouragement and inspiration as you venture into the unknown territory of entrepreneurship.

I remember feeling intimidated by the music business conference's teachers as if it were yesterday. By the time I got home that evening, I felt so defeated, and that was before my business had even gotten off the ground. I asked myself, "Am I really equipped to do this?"

That deceptive inner voice, imposter syndrome, planted seeds of doubt and insecurities. It told me that I was insufficiently qualified to teach and would never be able to match the expertise of my more experienced peers. For weeks, the thought of being discovered as a fraud plagued me, causing me to question my decision to become a music educator.

I was so close to throwing in the towel due to fear and not feeling qualified enough. *Nobody is going to take lessons from me. Who am I to teach kids? Unlike these other educators, I don't have a degree in music. Their bios are stacked with certifications, degrees, and experiences. What if I fail? How many people will approach me and say, "I told you so?" I knew it wouldn't work. You're insane for quitting your well-paying job to do what? Teach piano lessons?*

Yet, underneath it all, there was still a burning desire deep down, like an ember that would not die. I knew that my love of teaching and genuine ability to connect with children were two of my greatest strengths. I had my own teaching style and would bring a new perspective to music education. While my credentials may not have been impressive, I possessed something even more valuable—a tenacious faith in the transformative power of music.

Pushing through the fear and self-doubt, I continued running my business as a brand-new entrepreneur. I focused on what I could offer rather than what I lacked on paper. I devoted all my energy to creating a nurturing environment in my studio where every child feels seen, heard, and valued. I tailored my teaching methods to each student's needs, embracing their uniqueness and guiding them on their musical journey.

As my business grew, so did my confidence. Not only did I witness a change in my students (increased focus and self-confidence in lessons and outside of the studio) but so did their parents. The more you step out on faith and push through fear, my friend, the more you learn to defy fear. Recognizing my growth and my positive effect on children and their families helped me overcome my imposter syndrome and take advantage of new business opportunities.

But the most surprising twist in this story was yet to come. The same teachers who had once seemed so much more qualified on paper—the ones with PhDs and impressive accolades—started coming to me for advice. They recognized the results I was achieving with my students, the passion I instilled in them, and the positive energy that permeated my studio.

This realization was a pivotal moment in my life. It confirmed that, despite my doubts and insecurities, I had made the right decision when I launched the business. You see, academic credentials are not the sole determining factor in achieving entrepreneurial success; it's also about how much passion, dedication, and authentic connection we pour into our business.

Don't get me wrong; self-doubt and fear didn't disappear because of my success. Running a business has many ups and downs. Imposter syndrome leaves as your confidence grows, but what happens when your goals don't always go as planned and you experience failure?

Just when I thought my business was soaring, I faced setbacks and made mistakes. Instead of dwelling on them and letting imposter syndrome consume me, I transformed my shortcomings into valuable lessons. Each mistake taught me something new and allowed me to fine-tune my strategies and approach. The self-doubt that plagued me was alleviated by embracing failure as an integral part of the learning process.

One such setback was launching a music program that failed to acquire the traction I had anticipated. Even though I planned and prepared very carefully, the reaction was lukewarm, and I felt disheartened. But I didn't let this setback define me. Instead, I seized the opportunity to assess what went wrong and make adjustments to meet my clients' needs and preferences better. Because of this, I now view setbacks not as failures but as opportunities for growth and use them to drive me toward greater creativity and flexibility in my business.

I didn't know then that fear and self-doubt often indicate that we're stretching ourselves, pushing beyond our comfort zones, and embarking on something significant. It's a sign we're growing. So, rather than surrendering to fear, harness it as motivation to drive you forward.

Starting a business is a courageous act that requires facing your fears and overcoming self-doubt. Keep in mind your level of success in entrepreneurship is not solely dependent on your credentials and degrees. It is fueled by your enthusiasm and commitment to your work, as well as the impact you make and the lives you touch.

Looking back, I wish I had launched my business sooner. I wasted so many years believing I needed a degree, certifications on my wall, or accolades in my bio. I am sharing my lesson learned with you so that you may not waste any more time launching your business. If you take nothing else from this, remember that even the most successful business entrepreneurs have moments of fear and self-doubt.

In conclusion, when I finally dared to launch my business beyond my fears and doubts, I established a thriving music business and learned to trust in myself and my abilities. Embrace setbacks as learning opportunities, and, above all, take that first step. Even if impostor syndrome occasionally rears its ugly head, overcoming your fears can help you realize your true entrepreneurial potential.

Don't allow fear and self-doubt to paralyze you. Launch your business, face your fears head-on, and embrace the journey ahead. My friend, you've got this. I dare you to succeed!

ABOUT THE AUTHOR

Tonia Stoney is an energetic and passionate piano and music theory educator, composer, and mentor, specializing in teaching children at beginner and intermediate levels. With thirty years of experience, she brings an infectious energy to her teaching and genuinely loves working with kids. Tonia believes that playing the piano is similar to building with Legos, as each note helps to create a musical piece.

In addition to her dedication to music education, Tonia has a remarkable background. She served in the US Army and displayed superior leadership during combat operations, earning the Bronze Star Medal for her exceptional service.

Tonia's impact and accomplishments have garnered recognition. In 2015, Tonia established Music Is For Me, LLC, which received the Community Service Arts Award and was featured in South Carolina Voyager Magazine's Hidden Gem—Inspiring Stories Series. She has also been inducted into the Best of Summerville Business Hall of Fame for receiving the Best Piano Instructor Award for five consecutive years.

With her extensive teaching experience, infectious energy, military service, and composing abilities, Tonia Stoney is highly regarded in piano education and mentoring.

WILL KRALOVEC

The Shawshank Redemption is one of my favorite movies. It is a 1994 film adapted from Stephen King's novella *Rita Hayworth and Shawshank Redemption.* I like it for multiple reasons, but most of all because I see it as an allegory of life—at least the life that too many people unfortunately fall into. Whether or not Stephen King wrote the original novella as a metaphor for life, I know not.

The movie tells the story of banker Andy Dufresne, who is sentenced to life in prison for the double homicide of his philandering wife and her lover. Andy is sent to live out the rest of his life in Shawshank State Prison, even though he professes to being innocent of the murders.

Too many people, without knowing it, spend their lives in a Shawshank Prison of their own creation.

Society, parents, teachers, peers, employers, and others ingrain in our minds a definition of success in the United States that tends to emphasize financial attainment and the collecting of material things as the path to fulfillment, happiness, and joy. These, we are told repeatedly throughout life, will bring us status, security, comfort, and the people we desire in our lives.

Materialism, a focus singularly on financial gain, an independent go-it alone demeanor, and a fear-based mentality characteristic of our society can all conspire to put a new business owner into a self-made prison in which they become locked for life.

In the limited space of this one chapter, I cannot fully explain a philosophy of life and of how business should be orchestrated for the unique time in history in which we are living. For that, I am writing a whole book that will be published in the near future. It currently has a working title of *The Selfless Way in Business: A New Way of Thinking for a New Era.* It will be authored under my writing pseudonym, William A. Beacon. The book will explain a Selfless Business Model and the growth of social impact businesses around the globe, and why this growing sector of the business industry is going to have a considerable influence on business in general, as well as on society. (See Tip #3 below.)

Here are three business tips and one lesson learned from my business career that are applicable to *The Selfless Way in Business.* I hope these will help you better navigate your business future, and possibly even your future life choices, so both can provide you with much *authentic* fulfillment, happiness, and joy.

Tip 1: Values are to be used

People and businesses often profess to have strong values. But do they really?

Ask people, "Do you think having values is important in a person's life?"

And continue with, "What about a business; should it have its own core values?"

Then listen to the answers.

You will likely get treated to an earful of people spouting about the necessity for all people to have strong values. And likely, they too will extol the virtues of businesses needing to have strong values. You may even get a further lecture on people's disgust over companies not following their own stated values.

Then ask people, "What are your core values?"

"Huh, well, let me see…" will more than likely be similar to the answers you receive.

Unfortunately, this is a pretty typical scenario. And most companies are not much different. Ask the average employee to recite their company's core values, and the correct answers will be rare.

For most of my own adult life I have chosen to hold rather strong personal values. I review them about once a year, and occasionally tweak them as I have grown older and evolved over the years.

I have found, however, that this behavior is not the norm.

When I started or helped grow each of my past start-up or early growth companies, I made sure to instill each with a set of core values. These were not just intended as nice decorative window-dressing to give the appearance of being an upright corporate citizen. Rather, they were meant to be real, concrete, intentional, meaningful, and especially to be really applied on a daily basis. Values are to be used, not to be displayed collecting dust on a shelf. Having strong core values is a strong principle of living the Selfless Way in business.

If you strive to be a values-based person and run a values-based company start from day one. And don't compromise your values. You will sleep better at night, and you will garner greater respect and loyalty from your customers, suppliers, and employees. Which, overall, will translate into greater company reputation, stability, and even profitability.

Tip 2: Implementing the selfless way in business starts with self

You first must have a healthy relationship with yourself to have a good relationship with other people—especially your employees, customers/clients, suppliers, and all other company stakeholders. This is perhaps the first rule of living a Selfless Way in business.

It is all about maintaining work/life balance. You must take care of yourself to remain sharp, focused, and operating at the top of your game every day when you are growing your start-up company.

This involves prioritizing self-care.

It takes great strength, courage, discipline, and commitment to maintain a regular regiment of self-care. No matter how busy, stressed, or fatigued you become, you must attend to this daily. This should include prioritizing diet/nutrition, exercise, a full night's sleep, meditation, connections with people, time for spouse/partner and other family, devoting time to your passion/hobby/creative endeavors, and getting into nature regularly.

You also should have a morning routine. It is considered essential to have a one to two-hour self-care (and personal development) routine every morning as both a way to take care of yourself, and to establish the direction for the day. Waking up every morning and doing a routine of meditation, introspection, stretching, exercise, and personal growth (e.g., listening to inspirational podcasts, doing online trainings, journaling, etc.), along with writing down your exact intentions for the day are collectively one of the most powerful ways to attend to yourself and your business. The simple truth is, if you do not take care of yourself (especially during times of stress), you cannot take care of others. Your life, relationships, and ultimately your business will suffer if you do not.

Tip 3: Business should not be a zero-sum game

If you are like most people, you view the business world as a competition, something in which one side wins by a certain amount and the other side loses by an equivalent amount. In other words, you think business is a zero-sum game. This has been the prevailing mindset in the business world for a long time.

However, for one sector of business, this prevailing paradigm is rapidly changing.

Social impact businesses are helping cause this shift. Social impact businesses (some also call them "for-benefit companies") are collectively creating a new emerging "Fourth Sector" of the economy. The philosophy behind such businesses is changing one of the basic tenets of business that has existed since before the advent of modern capitalism was described by Adam Smith. For the first time in the history of business, something other than profit is taking priority—that is, social impact businesses are using business to create social good. This is a priority of equal or even greater focus than producing profit. This is significant not only for the future of business, but for society in general.

Social impact businesses are also not operating from the typical prevailing fear-based mentality where competition is revered within a zero-sum game mentality. Instead, social impact businesses are operating from a mindset of love and compassion, where collaboration and the belief in a win-win system has taken hold.

Fifty years ago, the notion of attaching the words love and compassion to business would have been heresy. Perhaps for many it still is. But consider the following.

Business competition, by its very nature, comes from a place of fear. It is based on a scarcity mindset. This makes us believe we must compete and ultimately beat our opponent, or else we will be robbed of our resources, suppliers, profits, market share, or whatever other metric a company uses to measure success. Holding on to a fear based mentality is not the best way to run your business, nor does it benefit society as a whole. This is true for a variety of reasons, which are mostly beyond the scope of this chapter to cover (but will be explained in the forthcoming book referenced at the beginning of this chapter).

On the other hand, operating instead from a place of love and compassion, where collaboration is preferred over competition, and a win-win mentality replaces the zero-sum game mentality, will benefit your business, as well as society. It has the potential to create even more abundance. Why? Because collaboration can cause more creativity, cooperation, and communications, which all can deliver greater profit.

All of these characteristics are part of operating from a Selfless Way in business.

My third business tip therefore is to adopt a Selfless Way mindset for your future business. If you do, you will not only align your future company and yourself with the shifts taking place both in business and society, but you will find more fulfillment, happiness, and joy in your work, and in your life.

Lesson Learned: Don't go it alone.

Many a new start-up business owners and entrepreneurs believe in going it alone, especially at the very beginning. Their reasons usually are one of the following justifications:

- I don't have the money to hire staff or outsource work.

- I can do it better than anyone else.

- No one else understands my business.

- My time is basically free, so I can spend my days (and weekends) doing work myself.

- How hard can it be? I'm smart, educated, driven, and focused. I got this!

- Everyone else started off with only themselves.

- If I can't depend on just me, then I shouldn't be in business.

- It's virtuous to work long, hard hours. It's a new business owner's baptism by fire.

- What would others think if I delegated responsibilities? Wouldn't I be seen as lazy or wasteful with money?

- My father or mother was a sole business owner. Going it alone was how they did it.

If one or more of the above fits your mindset, then you are not alone. Yet, you are in for a rude awakening. Each of the above reasons are faulty in today's business environment. Particularly if you desire to be an entrepreneur, rather than a business owner.

Let's clarify the difference between a business owner and an entrepreneur. A business owner starts a company to create a job for themselves, one in which their goal is usually to maximize revenue to the company, and in turn income to themself. This is a valid way to view a business start-up venture. But just know, in many cases, this job may become a proverbial prison from which one cannot escape. Your dream can instead turn into a nightmare of financial dependence on the business in which you are doing everything, working long hours, and forgoing time off or vacations. Not exactly the life you are envisioning for yourself, is it?

An entrepreneur, on the other hand, is seeking to create asset value, not revenue. Yes, the entrepreneur has to cover their living expenses, but once that is achieved, all excess cash is used to either grow the assets of the company or invest it in other ways to create other new assets. An eventual goal of the entrepreneur is to create multiple streams of passive income.

An entrepreneur does not desire to continue accumulating cash flow and hoard it away (other than perhaps the equivalent of three to six months of living expenses stashed away for an emergency). From day one, the entrepreneur is interested in putting processes and procedures in place that allow others to complete the work, independent of the entrepreneur overseeing every daily process. Eventually, the entrepreneur will fully staff the new company so it can operate on its own with only limited oversight from the entrepreneur.

The long-term goal of the entrepreneur is to spend their time working *on* their companies, not *in* their companies. Contrast this with the business owner who is working *in* their company, often for an entire career.

The latter harkens back to the opening of this chapter in which I mentioned my fondness of *The Shawshank Redemption* because I see it as an allegory for life. Too often, people seeking to create "the good life" end up creating and becoming a prisoner of their job for life. As the lead character says in the movie, you have to either, "Get busy living or get busy dying."

Do not become a prisoner to your job. And certainly, do not let it kill you because of overwork and stress. It's not a fun existence. Nor is it healthy. And frankly, it rarely brings great prosperity. You might make a decent living, but at what cost to the rest of your life?

Let me tell you a story about one of my past businesses. When I started it, I spent an inordinate amount of time learning how to create a website. I mean, a downright sick amount of time—six months or more. I believed that I had to create the perfect website for my new company and therefore decided I had to teach myself how to do it.

My reasons were many:

1. I did not feel I had the funds necessary to outsource the work

2. Explaining my new business model to outside service-providers would take too much time, and even then, people just would not understand how best to communicate it

3. I could do it all better myself

4. How hard could it really be?

5. Long hours were just a given in an entrepreneur's early journey. And so, at the time I felt all of these reasons were valid for "going it alone."

In hindsight, with many years of increased wisdom, it was a mistake. And frankly, that same mindset caused a series of similar mistakes, that in the long-run cost me time and money. A lot of time and money!

There's a curious thing about life, and about business. We often learn the most valuable lessons through what is sometimes referred to as the School of Hard Knocks. This school of hard knocks teaches that we experience the most profound lessons of life by way of enduring the pains of hardship, disappointment, struggles, and roadblocks.

This part of the school of hard knocks tends to be true. We can indeed learn a lot from these situations.

But there's another part of the school of hard knocks that is also prevalent. This is the image of the lone solitary maverick making their way in the world, facing every challenge head-on, as they slog forward by themself. This part of the storied school of hard knocks convinces many people that this is the best way to become an entrepreneurial success. Often, this person is held up as tough and gritty, street smart and seasoned, wise and hardened toward struggles, with knowledge well beyond their years.

But you know what? Do not buy into this part of the school of hard knocks. Its image of the go-it-alone, street-educated, self-made person has become nostalgic and quaint—it is no longer the best way to start and build a company, if it ever was. That is, if you want to be an entrepreneur instead of a business owner.

In today's business environment, the best way to accelerate your success, keep sanity and work/life balance (including staying married or in a relationship!), and even improve your quality and effectiveness is to collaborate with others. Standard business disciplines such as marketing, web design and maintenance, bookkeeping and accounting, administrative functions, etc. can all be handled by outside vendors, especially in today's digital and remote working environment. One might even end up having a marketing firm based in Seattle, a virtual assistant located in the Philippines, an accounting firm in Chicago, and various other vendors and suppliers scattered throughout the United States, and even the rest of the world.

And for God's sake, early on in a business start-up phase, hire a virtual assistant for at least a couple of hours a week to do necessary but mundane easy-to-accomplish administrative tasks. Otherwise, you will create a job that locks you into a prison, and eventually will bury you in so much work that you will be the first to enter in the morning and the last to turn off the lights in the evening, and on weekends. This is not the optimum future you should desire. Today's entrepreneur needs to build alliances, create partnerships, outsource responsibilities, and grow from collaboration. Heck, you may even eventually seek to collaborate with a competing company, in order to create more together than you can separately. The opportunities are endless.

Today, no one creates a company alone, and no entrepreneur creates multiple companies by themself. Collaboration is a core principle of the Selfless Way in business.

I wish you much success, balance in life, fulfillment, happiness, and joy from your business journey ahead. Best wishes!

ABOUT THE AUTHOR

Will Kralovec is a social entrepreneur, innovator, and vision-ary. He often pushes perceived limits seeking to make the impossible into the probable. He has three professional pri-orities that drive much of his work: people and improving the human condition, creation of the built-environment to be more people-centric, and social impact business and growing the "Fourth Sector."

Over nearly thirty years, Will has held leadership positions spanning all three economic sectors (private, government/public, and nonprofit). His professional experience includes work in real estate development, investment underwriting, finance, economic development, city planning, urban design, affordable housing, community development, and entrepreneurship.

During his career he has helped start or grow six early-stage companies. Today, Will runs JJK Places, PBC—a Denver based social impact real estate development company that uses real estate, space, and the built-environment to increase opportunity, community, wellness, and social equity, especially for historically underserved populations. Structured as a public benefit corporation (PBC) and Certified B Corp, JJK Places is one of the country's first "Fourth Sector" real estate development companies.

Will holds three master's degrees: an MBA from Cornell University, and a Master of Urban and Regional Planning, and a Master of Urban Design, both from the University of Colorado. He earned his Bachelor of Arts in History from the University of Vermont.

DANILA PALMIERI

My journey as an entrepreneur started in 2013 when I moved to the US because of my husband's job opportunity. At that time, I was working in Brazil as a consultant after leaving my corporate career and decided not to return but work for myself.

I did not plan much about the business or what I would provide as a service, although I knew I would like to work in the HR field with small companies. I had never really thought about building a company; I just wanted to serve others, be helpful, learn, and have fun.

Arriving in the US for the first time as a resident and looking for something to do was challenging. At the same time, I understood how to open a business and put together a business plan, and an opportunity knocked on my door.

Brazilian companies were coming to the US to invest, operate, or grow, and they needed someone to help them structure their operations, understand compliance, and build a team. That was when Connect Solutions was born as a boutique HR solution for international businesses, mainly from Brazil, doing business on American soil.

I was shy when I started but understood I needed to build relationships and be known locally. I knew my passion, my skills, and I knew I could deliver. I knew the language and the Brazilian culture, but I had much to learn about the US and workforce law and relations. Basing my strategy on "learn as we go," I engaged with a CPA boutique company focused on transborder transactions between Brazil and the US. I started work while learning from associations such as SHRM, the Brazilian-American Chamber of Commerce, and the WTC Atlanta, among other educational programs at SBA.

I created a hobby from learning, working, and making money to reinvest in my knowledge and exposure, but I needed to build a business. I could not live off my work. At the same time, my daughter was born, and I also needed to learn how to be a mother, a business owner, a wife, and other roles we perform in life. We could not focus on building a business from the ground up, so I chose to be a mother and keep my hobby as an entrepreneur. Don't think I gave up! I was learning from my clients and pushing myself to keep building relationships and be known as a professional in the US, but my primary job was to be a mother, not create a business.

I doubled my revenue each year of my daughter's first three years of life, which were good results since I was only working with referrals and word-of-mouth projects. You might be wondering how I did that. I'm an excellent closer and had a 99% rate conversion from my CPA Partner's referrals.

That wasn't enough, and I wanted to create a business, grow, build a legacy, make money, and become a millionaire. Why not? I used to be independent in Brazil, and I wanted to have all that again and prove I could make it.

I was hungry to build something great, and I could do it. Here is where I learned the tips I'm sharing with you. They helped me overcome fears, innocence, paralysis, and trust in myself.

Tip 1: Focus or Fail

> *"Your past does not define you.*
> *It prepares you."*
> —Darren Hardy

Between 2019 and 2022, I decided to be a superwoman and diversify my business by targeting different markets and providing a brother list of services.

I turned my company into a one-stop-shop solution focusing on companies with a growth strategy that were planning to reach a new market, acquiring new companies, or looking for investments. I was hungry for growth and thought I would be able to take a big step forward.

I found someone with the same ambitions, and that was all we needed. We built a plan, used part of our savings, believed we could, and took the leap. Two years later, I was reinventing my company and myself.

My growth venture failed mainly because I was shooting everywhere and picking the next shining opportunity without closing past ones. We were able to connect with critical targets and build partnerships, and we were able to bring a team to support, but we lacked focus; I was unable to align the team to an objective and convert the results necessary to inject cash flow and sustain the business.

Coming from a corporate experience, I tried to apply concepts and methodologies, bring good professionals, and act as a corporation, but we were not one, and the lack of focus killed my dream to grow fast.

In 2022, after learning that focus was necessary for survival, sustainability, and growth, I decided to end that venture and start over, returning to my previous business and focus: HR services for international companies in the US.

This time I evaluated my strengths, weaknesses, reputation, expertise, deliverables, partnerships, relationships, and priorities and relaunched my business, focusing on opportunities in my field of knowledge, recognition, and experience.

I doubled the company's size in twelve months and reached my annual goal in the first quarter of 2023—all because I focused.

My recipe for success was:

1. Define your market opportunity and customer persona and find your blue ocean.

2. Create the results you want to achieve in the short term. I chose 12 months, breaking into small goals each quarter.

3. Reconnect with your audience by clarifying your message.

4. Become part of the community you serve and, share your knowledge, become the authority in your field.

5. Invest in yourself and reinvest in your company.

Go out there, and don't let your past define you. Learn from failure, and don't be afraid to jump into another chance to learn something new and succeed.

Tip 2: Trust yourself

> *"Follow your instincts. That's where*
> *true wisdom manifests itself."*
>
> —Oprah Winfrey

I came from a low-class Brazilian family with blue-collar jobs living paycheck to paycheck. When I was seven years old, my parents lost their jobs, and we moved to my grandparent's house. I cannot imagine how difficult it was for my parents to reinvent themselves and start over while raising a seven and a three-year-old. My mom was always a fighter and still is. She became a hairdresser, then a dental prosthetist, managed a nonprofit, and graduated years later as a psychologist. My dad sold magazines, worked as a watchmaker, sold cars, graduated from college in business, became a teacher at the university, and retired a couple of years ago.

I spent my childhood dreaming of having a big house, a fancy car, and traveling the world. I was tired of seeing my parents living paycheck to paycheck, managing credit card debts and loans. My dream was to have enough money that I didn't need to worry about counting and stretching my budget to buy a pair of pants. I dreamed of being independently wealthy.

Because of my mom, I graduated as an engineer from one of the best universities in Brazil. I had good jobs and worked hard to become a leader. I came from a family with entrepreneurship skills. My granddad had a barber shop for fifty years, and my uncle has one of the best restaurants in the city where I was born. I thought I wasn't built for it, that I was meant for corporate life—until I reached the last step in the ladder.

In 2012, everything changed in my corporate life, and in 2013 I moved to the US because of my husband's job and became an entrepreneur, founding my HR practice and focusing on Brazilian companies doing business in the US.

I always dreamed of living abroad, living a different life from the one I already knew, and experiencing another way of seeing the world, values, and culture. I never dreamed of living here in the US, but it was and still is an excellent gift of the universe.

The first thing I did when I put my foot on the ground was to learn English. I already knew some but needed to be more fluent. My strategy was to embrace and adapt and learn a new culture. I could not be only a wife supporting my husband's new job; I had to do something about my own professional life, too.

I have the same fire in my belly as my mom. I learned from her never to give up, to foster my dreams, and to be independent. I decided not to return to the corporate world when I moved to this country. My dream wasn't only to make money but live purposefully, doing something I liked and related to my passion: people, processes, and business.

Why HR? During my corporate career, I was terrific at choosing and developing people. It was also easy to manage projects, design a more efficient process and support other businesses in achieving their goals. I am result-driven. I can only sleep well if my clients are getting more than expected, so I deliver excellence.

I founded my HR practice in 2013, based on an opportunity to serve Brazilian companies doing business in the US. Since 2009, Brazilian companies have been increasingly looking to expand to the US market to become international or diversify beyond Latin America.

This opportunity came when the CPA company I hired to open my company in the US, who served this market, wanted me to support their clients with HR services. I did not think twice. I jumped to grab this opportunity and rushed to learn all about HR in America.

I am fortunate to have built a business that provides knowledge, expertise, resources, and a hands-on approach to companies navigating a new ocean of opportunities. Over this first decade as an entrepreneur, I had my pitfalls, doubted myself, questioned my gut, and sometimes trusted more in others than myself. Understanding the struggle is part of the growth process, be flexible, keep your eyes on the horizon, know where you are going, embrace and adapt toward change and opportunities, and be happy.

Tip 3: Dream big and keep your feet on the ground

"Your ability will grow to match your dreams."

–Jim Rohn

When I look back to my childhood and teenage years, I feel I have everything I dreamed of. Should I have dreamed bigger?

Never stop dreaming! You are what you dream, and the universe will conspire to it, but keep your feet on the ground because nothing will come easy. You need to work hard.

I dreamed big once, bigger than my ability to accomplish the goals I designed in a certain period. The problem wasn't my dream; the problem was the timeline mixed with incompetence and lack of expertise. I built a sandcastle, which luckily fell apart before it was too difficult to clean up the mess.

My mom always taught me the power of the subconscious, the power of believing, and the need to implement a plan and take action. I've been applying concepts I learned from Napoleon Hill and Joseph Murphy, along with Jim Rohn and Darren Hardy. You can be whatever you want if you are flexible, open to learning constantly, and work smart and very often hard.

I doubled my company in twelve months because I applied a few concepts:

1. How big is my dream for that period?

2. What skills do I need to learn or must have?

3. How much time will I commit or can I commit to achieve?

4. What investment, resources, and relationships do I have or need to create?

5. What are my strengths and weaknesses?

6. What is my action plan? What steps do I have to take to get there?

I am practical, straightforward, and results-driven. The mentors I have chosen have given me tools, forms, and handouts to follow through. What worked for me was working on my journal every day to move one step forward toward my goals, applying and focusing on the tasks I must make, and committing time to it.

My secret receipt was always discipline, and consistency, every day, one step at a time.

Lesson Learned: Embrace and Adapt

"Once you stop learning, you start dying."
—Albert Einstein

My first boss would say to me, "Learn, even if it's how *not* to do it." That was my first professional lesson, but it applied to my life. Learn at every opportunity.

These past ten years of entrepreneurship have taught me the power of discipline, focus, flexibility, adaptation, and the ability to decide quickly and let it go to transform yourself and your business. Also, failing was part of my growth path, a painful way to learn. Still, if you have compassion for yourself, mourn your loss, and move forward rapidly, I guarantee you will be stronger and well-prepared for growth, conquer your next goal, and overcome your next challenge easier. We cannot always win, but we can mitigate risk by investing time in planning, analyzing the moment, and taking that calculated risk.

As you know, I arrived in the US from Brazil from a high-level corporate career. I had the option to hold a similar job here, but I decided to open a business in a place with a brand-new culture, language, professional etiquette, and ways to negotiate and do business. I had to learn fast. Some things took time and are still ongoing while others were very easy. Sometimes I felt I did not belong because ten years is not enough to learn five hundred years of a country's history and customs. I also have a Brazilian background that differentiates me from other professionals and entrepreneurs in the US and Brazil. I can navigate both worlds and have transformed them as strengths and part of my business—the power of adaptation, discipline, and flexibility.

Another important lesson is to control your ambition. Ambition is good and gives you energy, motivation, and direction, but do not bite off more than you can chew. How do you eat an elephant? One bite at a time. Keep that in mind. Becoming an entrepreneur is like taking a rollercoaster ride with ups and downs, brutal and unexpected shifts, twists, falls, and turns with much joy, some headaches, and a few stomachaches. If you learn from it, persist, and prepare yourself for the next, anticipating the problems, the ride becomes smoother and more pleasant.

Remember, we can have everything we want, just not simultaneously. It is a process of acquiring part at a time. Life is short, so don't waste time doing something just for money. Be passionate about it and leave a legacy; invest your time creating something good for yourself, your loved ones, and your community. Make an impact and live well and prosper.

ABOUT THE AUTHOR

Danila brings over twenty years of experience in financial services, manufacturing, mining, and metals companies in Brazil, Latin America, and the United States. She worked with companies such as Experian, Votorantim Metais, and Braskem in Brazil. She has extensive experience implementing projects to evaluate, analyze and improve business strategies. She served as Human Resources and Organizational Development

Manager in Brazil. She helped lead M&A processes in Latin America and Brazil, working to integrate the cultures of the acquired companies.

In 2013, she moved to the US and founded Connect Solutions, intending to support Brazilian companies operating in the US. She focused on strategic management planning, organizational development, recruitment and selection, employee relations, compliance, American labor law, and adaptation to the local culture. In Atlanta, she was part of the Brazilian American Chamber of the Southeast USA team for seven years and chairman for one year. She served for five years as WTC Atlanta board member.

She holds an MBA in Business Management with an emphasis on human resources from Fundação Getúlio Vargas, São Paulo, Brazil, and a Bachelor's Degree in Chemical Engineering from the Faculty of Industrial Engineering, São Paulo, Brazil. Financial Management from Emory University, Startup Funding from Cambridge University, Customer Service Experience from George Washington University, and is currently studying the Chief Human Resources Officer Program at the Wharton University of Pennsylvania.

TIA CRISTY

Tip 1: Consistency is Key

I can't recall the first time I heard the phrase "consistency is key" or who first said it, but I'm sure you've heard some similar words from authors and speakers like John Maxwell or Tony Gaskins over the years. So honestly, it doesn't matter who said it first; when something is very good, it will withstand the test of time.

The concept is simple, but it can be taken too broadly. Consistency is essential when developing good habits. Building your business takes consistency. However, what specifically needs consistency can change over time. When I started "Tips from Tia," I consistently focused on typing as many tips as possible on a given day. It was like writing down recipes. I wasn't focused on perfection in the presentation but on recording the most accurate tips that genuinely worked. Today, it isn't about getting as many tips on the site as possible but about having the proper format for analytics. I take time to zero in on more of the background needs, ...And I cannot forget to stress about the social links.

But why is consistency so important? Because if you lose rhythm, you can lose traction. For example, I built up my following on Instagram after incorporating a daily regimen of posts for about twelve months. After hitting a good number, I set my sights on something else and didn't post for two months. Unfortunately, I got a hard lesson in consistency. Over five thousand audience members left me because I neglected them for sixty days. Five thousand people may not be so painful when you have over a million followers, but it makes a massive dent if you're swimming in the tens of thousands. Imagine if you only had five thousand followers and you lost them all. And yes, losing loyal audience members can be devastating, but remember that without being consistent, to your audience, you become the unreliable one.

Tip 2: Be Yourself

Every impactful lesson in life reminds us that self-love is needed before anyone else can love you. It might sound false when you see self-deprecating folks in relationships, but are those relationships truly based on unconditional love? Love with conditions can be exhausting. So many other things in life can be exhausting, so why not set a proper foundation of unconditional love for yourself? Loving yourself doesn't mean you're perfect or think you're the best at everything, or you will never have a self-doubting moment. But when you love yourself, oddities and all, you can confidently be yourself. And as Oscar Wilde said it best, *"...Everyone else is already taken."*

You'll hear the word "authentic" thrown around a lot in business. However, don't let the overuse of the word turn you off from being authentic. Authenticity is imperative to be successful. Authentic doesn't mean you must develop a unique product that no one has ever seen. Perhaps, you'll be authentic by putting a refreshing twist on a traditional product.

Nevertheless, authenticity is all about being truthful and genuine. So even if you create a new version of an age-old product, you have a greater chance of success if you and your company are honest since honest people are considered trustworthy. For example, upon launch, people might be initially attracted to your product, but if you handle your business without authenticity, you will not gain loyal customers, readers, or followers.

In the past, most people would take the first-place listing on the search engine as trustworthy solid gold. However, we've learned just because a company had enough money to win the bid for the top listing on page one of the search engine, the result didn't always guarantee authentic information.

In the case of "Tips from Tia," my mission from out the gate was to be a trusted resource on lifestyle tips because I was tired of searching the web and getting the wrong answer because it was the first thing that popped up. Today, search engines are constantly adjusting algorithms to accommodate business authenticity while highlighting those paid 'Ad Results'. So, the story's moral is that by being authentic and honest with your target audience, you will have a better chance of gaining a loyal customer base and keeping them in the long run.

Tip 3: Finding the Right Team

Picking the right team to help you achieve your vision is the most critical decision you will make in business. Nobody will love your business, creation, or baby as much as you will. Still, if you are a good leader, a servant leader, and an overall good human being, there's a great chance your employees will love your business like a distant cousin or some other treasured family member. Your business might be a significant aspect of your life, but it's only a way for employees to create a good life for themselves. So, you want to let your employees know that you care about them and their life. Take time to discover who they are and where their passions lie. Think about it this way, aren't you more apt to help someone you believe cares about you? Of course. We are all built that way. So, get to know those who help bring your vision to life.

Another vital thing to remember is to be aware of your weaknesses. Picking team members who are strong where you are weak is what will help your business excel. I like to say, *"I want to be good, but I don't have to be good at everything. That's why I also rely on knowing good people."*

Lesson Learned: Don't Let Stubbornness Be Ignorance

I was today years old the last time I had to remind myself, don't let stubbornness be ignorance. Yes, I have to retell myself this regularly when new opportunities arise that may or may not benefit my business. Let me first say that being stubborn isn't always a bad thing. There's a fine line where being stubborn can be courageous because even the definition states "determination" as its supreme quality. Unfortunately, "stubborn" also says that determination, in this case, cannot be waivered regardless of sound reasoning, which means that stubbornness can bite you hard at times. I'm happy to announce that stubbornness isn't a primary character trait of mine. However, it happens to all of us now and then.

When I was a child in my single digits, and adults would ask me what I wanted to be when I grew up, I would say either a lawyer or a hairdresser. The grownups would chuckle and say, "How adorable." However, I didn't see the contrast between the two professions as grownup eyes did. By the age of fourteen, I worked summers with a fabulous stylist who taught me the ins and outs of hair fashion while working as her resident shampoo girl. I learned a lot but also discovered it wasn't my passion. Sure, it was great giving top-notch advice to the customers on what to use on the hair or skin, but it was challenging for me to get past other people's thrill for gossip. And I say, without judgement, gossip seemed to be a prerequisite to being successful at the job. However, I was stubborn about spending my time reading the gossip rags. It wasn't my cup of tea. Plus,

I wasn't good at the concept. Whenever I attempted gossip, I asked people if they had seen the latest documentary on the history channel or had read any good books lately. I got good at knowing details about music artists because I had a love for music. Still, I was at a loss when it came to other celebrities, unless they were jumping on Oprah's couch or on the cover of the magazines we had spread across the salon coffee table. Yet, I was missing out on some money opportunities due to my stubbornness since the gossipy interaction, in fact, helped increase the tips I'd receive. But I ask, did knowing this stuff make me a better human? Probably, not.

I loved knowing how to cut and style, if only to save myself and my family money when it came to having great hair, but it pained me to know that all the fruitless interaction didn't fulfill me. So, studying law became the next step in my search for my passion.

By the time college rolled around, I was in the grove of taking pre-law classes while working at one of the top local salons, still working the wash bowl, and making a more conscious effort to use my strengths by giving clients excellent tips on hair care rather than discussing who was in the news that week. It turns out I was excellent at providing tips, and I was good at studying the law. But unfortunately, the law didn't bring me the warm and fuzzy feelings I hoped for. I was winning arguments in class but feeling guilty afterward. I loved the research but felt icky when I put it into practice.

This time I became courageously stubborn. I was stubborn about taking on practice cases that I knew could win only by what I felt was sacrificing my core values. I began refusing to take on the easy wins that weren't positively benefiting the planet because I figured in the future, if I were to do this as a profession, no money on earth was worth the feeling of evil that taunted me afterward. The undesired pressure was building inside me like a combustible pile of cinders about to burst at any moment.

I needed a creative outlet. I needed to spread joy. So, I found happiness in DJing. I knew the music. I loved music, and thanks to my salon gig, I absorbed the latest gossip about the artists I was playing. I was able to relay those nuggets when I'd get on the mic to announce the next song or the night's drink specials.

I was a busy young adult between my classes, the salon, and spinning the hottest music in nightclubs. The accumulation of what I was doing made me feel emotionally satisfied, but I was draining my most precious resource, time. Little did I know, I was on the verge of burnout and had no clue what I was supposed to be doing with my life.

Alone, none of the career choices in front of me felt completely rewarding. Still, when I tallied up the most remarkable aspects of each of the things I was doing, I realized it wasn't about the job title but by specific objectives in each job that contained something I loved. It became apparent I wanted to help people, first and foremost. I wanted to make a positive impact in the world. I wanted to give advice and make people's lives easier. And I wanted to be entertaining and bring happiness to others while doing it all. Unfortunately, there was no exact occupation I could find that fit the bill. That is until the first vehicle of my destiny showed up.

When DJing a happy hour at one of Philly's hottest nightclubs, I never expected that I would get discovered by a radio program director. Without getting into the whole nitty-gritty or a step-by-step timeline, I entered the world of radio broadcasting. It was the closest I had come to reaching that all-encompassing feeling of driving passion. Finally, I found a way to help people through a highly respected platform while incorporating entertainment. It was practically perfect for a long time.

As social media hit the scene, wreaking havoc on society by causing cyberbullying and philandering to be effortless for people, I grew stubborn from partaking since I suspected the bad outweighed the good. Plus, I believe I wouldn't stick around too long. I thought it was a trend like MySpace and would eventually fade into the background. But, to my surprise, newer social media caught fire and became a household staple. It became one of the best ways to spread positive messages, advertise, and connect with specific demographics.

My stubbornness with social media wasn't an all-or-nothing, which was probably another mistake. I would dip a toe into the social media pool and pull back out like the water was freezing. For example, I finally gave in to having a Facebook profile. However, unless it had to do with work, I wasn't posting. When Instagram launched, I was highly opposed to posting pictures for the world to critique. Is vanity ever a positive message? By the way, or BTW, 'No', is always the correct answer. But did I misjudge Instagram as a whole? Probably.

When I started "Tips from Tia," I realized social media wasn't going anywhere because it was *everywhere*. Even companies like senior citizen homes and daycares had social media pages. I realized I had better collect the specific handles for my site. I plucked @TipsfromTia on everything I could, and I'm glad I at least had the foresight to do this because, eventually, posting became inevitable.

As other influencers had hundreds of thousands or even millions of followers, I was starting from scratch. I had plenty of readers and thousands upon thousands of subscribers on my site, but I had to build a reputation through a different kind of platform, one that I had no passion for, or, at the time, respect for.

I'm a researcher by character, so I started researching the good of social media since I was already aware of its bad and ugly sides. For starters, advertising a company's best traits was a brilliant and inexpensive way. Next, it was a great resource to target demographics and psychographics. Finally, it was a way to connect old and new. And the more I learned, the more I had a softer side opinion on social media.

As "Tips from Tia" increased in popularity online, I started getting sponsors who wanted social media posts. I dreaded this in the beginning. I didn't have a substantial following on social, and I still wasn't particularly convinced I wanted one either since social media was still causing lots of commotion in the world through catfishing, identity stealing, and the newest ways to scam people. Not to mention, the constant creepy 'poking' and 'waves' from strangers on the daily.

One day, I posted an article from "Tips from Tia" on Facebook about getting pen stains out of leather. I got a direct message from a woman stating that she had tried a dozen things she had found online to use on her new couch, and my tip was the only thing that worked. I instantly remembered why I do what I do. My "Why" is to help others cut through the wrong information and get the trusted tip.

It's been said in many variations and by many great educators, including Mahatma Gandhi, "Be the change you want to see in this world."

I realized I could do good things with social media and reach a different audience. From that point, I began to respect social media like any other tool that could be used for good or bad, and I would choose to use it for good. I nixed my stubbornness little by little to provide a gift to others. I stopped focusing on the numbers and looked to do what I do best—helping others. That's when I finally began to gain real traction in social media.

It's still not easy today as I continue to fight my stubbornness with each new platform I join, but it's a consistent work in progress. The biggest thing is that I remain true to my brand. I won't ever jump on a negative trend to move the needle. I know my brand, and so do those that follow it. So why would I risk their loyalty to gain a few fleeting followers?

I'm all for shaking up material or incorporating something new, but I stick to my core values. By doing that, I know I'll be able to be proud of myself whether it succeeds or not. If something new fails, at least, I failed forward.

I recognized that I could still be stubborn after all these years when I was recently approached to do a podcast. I have been against doing podcasts for over a decade. But now, I have an opportunity to do a podcast the way I would want to do a podcast. I'm not sure what I'll decide, but whatever I choose, I will own my decision and learn from it. Because, in full transparency, I've had to pivot with the times and trends over the years. Still, sometimes I wonder where I'd be or how much farther along I would be today if I had taken on every request when the trends were in their infancy before they grew into household names. However, I then remember who I am, my core values, and my beliefs and thank God for his perfect timing because I'm well aware that my timing can suck, and so can my resistance to things.

As I grow in audience size, and, more importantly, in mindset, I'm learning it's vital to know the difference between saying 'No' because you feel it in your gut or if you're simply saying 'No' because you are just trying not to jump off the bridge like everyone else.

So, yes! Go ahead and be stubborn when you must but remember to ask yourself if your stubbornness leads you to ignorance or bravery.

ABOUT THE AUTHOR

I am a personality and tips expert in health and beauty through radio, television, and print. I continue learning every day so I can provide trusted and accurate information to others. I read medical journals for fun. I cheer on others so that people might continue to push themselves to be the best they can be and inspire me in return.

I have been under the umbrella of writing my entire life. Since the start of my career, specializing in words, I've contributed to newsprint, local magazines, web, scripts, copy, and manuscripts. Today, I also help others with their words by ghostwriting and teaching voice. My favorite thing about what I do is making others feel special. I have the unique opportunity to make someone's day slightly better by what I say. And I take that very seriously.

In 2012, my tips blog site, TipsfromTia.com, was launched. Now, with over one million unique visitors and 100k+ subscribers and followers on social media like Facebook, Twitter, Pinterest, and Instagram, I am grateful to share my knowledge on living a better lifestyle.

TipsfromTia.com won Best Blog for Wellness and Beauty–USA for 2020 and 2022. It has also been nominated for a prestigious Webby Award, a Lovie Award, and two UK Blog Awards, all in the Best Lifestyle and Best Beauty blog categories.

I know the importance of being a brand. I want to be known as a trusted resource for my readers and followers. I am honored to be an alum speaker for the TEDx Women's Conference and winner of Most Influential Lifestyle Businesswoman 2023.

TONYA BAYNES

Tip 1: Be selective when building relationships. Ask yourself: Will I still like them in 10 years?

Do either of these phrases ring a bell?

"Surround yourself with individuals who are smarter and more successful than you."

"If you want to go fast, go alone; if you want to go far, go with others."

Here's one that strongly resonates with me: "Be mindful of the company you keep."

When starting a business, it's easy to get caught up and become influenced by experienced entrepreneurs who seem to be killing it or by well-intentioned people eager to help you. When I started my entrepreneurial journey, I wanted to meet with anyone who was a coach, anyone who had some secret sauce to share with me, and frankly, anyone who could offer a guiding hand.

I met numerous people and expanded my network, but only a few remained in my life long-term. The ones who made the cut are those who made the most positive impact. They showed up when I was uncertain and clueless, offering me invaluable advice, feedback, and encouragement to keep going. They are diligently, tirelessly working on their businesses day in and day out, making mistakes and sharing the lessons along the way.

They check in on me once in a while, expressing genuine concern for my well-being. They introduce me to like-minded people who share my interests. They engage with my posts and send articles and media that support my work.

In business, relationships are crucial because the right connections can help your business grow and guide you along the right path. They do not hesitate to point out when you're making mistakes, delivering subpar work, or doing something that's just plain dumb. They support and share your launches and assist you as best as possible.

Which is not always monetary.

At the end of my first year in business, I held a strategic planning session for the upcoming year. I invited eight of the most successful women I knew. These women were not all millionaires, some did not even own businesses, but they were exceptional in their respective fields. I spent hours creating an agenda, fine-tuning my vision and mission statements, and drafting my S.M.A.R.T. goals. Ten minutes into the meeting, they were crossing things out, shaking their heads no, and pretty much doing air shots in the trash with my handouts. It turned out to be the most valuable meeting I ever had!

If the people around you aren't motivating, inspiring, or contributing to your expansion, it's time to reevaluate your circle of influence.

Finally, although technology has made networking and connecting with others more accessible, building lasting relationships remains a skill that requires time and effort. The most fruitful and successful relationships thrive on reciprocity, where both parties actively participate and invest in the connection.

Tip 2: Seize the day and the week by mastering your calendar

Deciding to become an entrepreneur is not a decision most make casually. One of the biggest initial mistakes is under-estimating how much time we will spend working on and in the business. And if you are like the rest of the world, you probably have other personal, family, or health obligations that will take up significant chunks of your time.

As a business owner, especially if you're a solopreneur in the service industry, your calendar becomes one of your most valuable tools—your personal almanac. Every aspect of your life, from business and personal commitments to family engagements, should be habitually recorded in your calendar.

And when I say calendar, I'm talking about a digital calendar. You can access one from your phone or computer, preferably synced to both, and if it's connected to your primary email address, even better. I'm sorry (not sorry) to tell you; it's time to retire the paper. Yes, I said it, and I'm talking to you. A planner is not a calendar, so by all means, keep your paper planners. Calendars and planners support each other, but they have different purposes. I'm talking about knowing where you need to be and what you must be doing at all times, especially if it's self-care, like reading a book in the park.

Yes, you will need to schedule time to read. You should also schedule driving time, non-appointment work time, gym time, morning routine time, buffer between meetings time, and anything else that requires your physical presence during the day.

Add restricted times to your schedule that you can dedicate to deeply focusing on a project or other essential tasks. And if you are really busy, schedule time to eat.

Everything that is happening, every place I'm supposed to be, every meeting I'm attending (or tentatively attending), and every project I'm working on are all entered into my calendar.

Every doctor's appointment, every gym workout, every coffee with a friend. It's all there. Period. Beautifully laid out and color-coded like a rainbow Tetris.

Consider using different colors for different aspects of your life. I use yellow for business, orange for personal, blue for family, and green for health. Another idea is to color code for varying priority levels.

Why be so meticulous with scheduling every minute, you ask? It's simple—time is your most precious resource. There will always be more work to do, but we all have the same 168 hours a week, and it cannot be renewed. So make sure you are the master of your time and schedule yourself first because once you give it away, it is gone forever.

Tip 3: Fall in love with automation and outsourcing; it's a form of business self-care

A while back, some popular social media reels were created by small business owners. The videos would begin with the caption "Meet the Team" and then show the solopreneur enacting all the tasks they perform for their business with corresponding job titles. Some were quite entertaining, showing owners in various rooms of their homes in different changes of clothing representing the different roles, topped with the dramatically increasing levels of exhaustion that come with each additional responsibility.

If I were to create a reel for my business, it would be super short, with one frame showing me sitting at my desk on a mock virtual call with the caption: Coach.

Yes, as a business owner, I have the responsibilities of bookkeeping, paying bills, marketing, social media, customer service, admin, and more, but I don't have to do any of them—I outsource and automate them.

Outsourcing is the act of subcontracting a function of your business. It ensures an expert executes tasks out of your wheelhouse or knowledge base. I'm an excellent coach, but if I had to do my bookkeeping, I'd be in big trouble every year at tax time.

Automation is the use of technology to perform manual tasks. Automation can increase productivity and help streamline your most time-consuming tasks. I automate my business's social media posts, newsletters, auto-respond emails, and bills.

Both of these tools save you money and time and provide greater flexibility to focus on the bigger picture of your business. They allow you to prioritize the goals that will help you bring your business vision to fruition.

I would encourage you not to fall into the trap of thinking that you can't afford to outsource. You can't afford *not* to! There are tons of high-quality, lower-cost options. Where I live, a woman-owned accounting company will do pro bono work for women-owned businesses that make under a certain income threshold. There is also a plethora of software that can get the job done.

I would also recommend outsourcing and automating most things in your personal life to free up your time there. I outsource my cleaning and shopping and use automation to pay bills and replenish our most commonly used household items.

Finally, to be crystal clear, outsourcing and automating doesn't mean you can completely wash your hands of all tasks. It is your business, after all. You must put in the effort to set things up and find the best provider to hire or subscribe to. Then, of course, there will be periodic maintenance. However, the time you spend upfront will create a high level of efficiency that will save you countless hours to do more things that matter.

Lesson Learned: Hire a coach or get yourself a committed mentor and listen to them—like yesterday

I am a life coach with an unwavering belief in the power of personal transformation. Life coaching has meant recognizing that every human possesses a unique set of strengths and values that can help them achieve their dreams. These characteristics can empower people to go deep within themselves to overcome their challenges and create meaningful change.

I started my coaching business wide-eyed and full of extraverted eagerness. No niche, no real plan, only armed with a Zoom account, my new fancy certificate, and a heart full of empathy. I was confident in my coaching abilities and was determined to feed my passion for helping others. I was convinced my innate talent and dedication would be enough to lead me toward success.

I secured a dedicated desk at a local coworking space so I would have a place to go outside of my home where I could focus. I hired a photographer to capture me in action during my working hours. I used the prints to build a website and start several social media pages. Now I was really in business! Slowly clients began to trickle in, and I poured everything into each session, listening intently, asking great questions, and giving them valuable insights and strategies to make their desired changes. This was an incredibly rewarding time, and I knew I was creating something special.

However, as the weeks turned into months, the initial excitement faded. I realized that while I was great at coaching, my earlier enthusiasm overshadowed a crucial piece of my business—the business itself.

Like most entrepreneurs, I didn't go into business to do business. I became an entrepreneur because I wanted to impact people's lives, to help people find the best versions of themselves, to co-create a path leading to their own definitions of success. I did not come here to run a social media marketing empire nor to create countless rows in accounting spreadsheets, and I was definitely not in it for hours of scheduling meetings in my calendar.

I found myself grappling with the realities of running a business. I had no idea building a thriving company would be so challenging. Realizing there was so much more to it than simply being a great coach, my business began to feel like work.

The administrative tasks piled up, and I struggled to balance working with clients and executing the operations side of things. I couldn't help but feel overwhelmed and stretched way too thin. I was juggling countless responsibilities and barely keeping up. The passion and energy that had initially fueled me were depleting fast. Doubts began to creep in. Was I cut out for this? Did I have what it took to build a thriving coaching practice?

It was clear to me that I had to do something different. Something that I had not already thought of. A decision needed to be made. So I made the most logical decision I could. I thought, *Duh! I'm a coach*! *I'll just coach myself through it like any of my clients.*

I'll give you one guess as to how that turned out.

It did not take long to realize that I was doing a poor job of coaching myself. Don't get me wrong; I believe we can coach ourselves through hard times and tricky situations. We do it every day. I also believe a dentist could fill her own cavities, but I'm not convinced that's the best option.

I needed a coach.

A coach to coach the coach.

Around this time, an old colleague and I reconnected on LinkedIn. We were both getting our businesses off the ground, and she shared with me a program she had just finished with a communications coach named Jen, who lived in London. I told her I needed a business coach, but she was adamant I needed Jen.

She was right. Jen's program was first-rate. She was instrumental in helping me create the signature programs I now use to create transformative experiences for my clients. She helped me find my voice and say what I meant, and she pushed me far out of my comfort zone. Years later, her lessons still ring true, and I have grown more assured in the power of my words.

I had clearer messaging and a secret sauce to entice potential clients, but I was still drowning in the business side of things.

Finally, fate intervened. I attended a breakfast networking event and serendipitously sat at a table with Steve, a business coach specializing in helping entrepreneurs like me. We struck up a conversation, and he shared his insights and experiences. He talked about systems, automation, and strategies that could simplify my business and allow me to focus on what I did best—coaching. I took that as a loud, cymbals-crashing sign, and without hesitation, he was hired.

On our first call, he asked me to grab a blank sheet of paper and divide it into nine squares, two lines down, two lines across, like a tic-tac-toe board. He then asked me nine questions, and I put the answers in each corresponding square. An hour later, when we were done, he said okay, here is your new business and marketing plan.

It took me a second to realize what I was looking at, but there it was, neatly laid out in front of me. My goals leaped from the page, and I knew precisely what I needed to do to grow my business. We mapped out my high-level goals for the rest of the year and the remaining quarters in only one hour. I immediately felt a pang of regret for not intentionally seeking out a business coach sooner.

Over the next few weeks, we built a comprehensive business plan and refined my target market. After a couple of months, we created a brand that authentically reflected who I was and what I offered. We established new systems for client management, scheduling, and financial tracking. Steve introduced me to technology that simplified my administrative tasks, freeing up valuable time for me to focus on my clients and my professional growth. A heavy weight lifted off my shoulders.

My newfound clarity and business insight allowed me to support those who entrusted me with their goals and dreams even better. Bottom line: I was becoming a better coach.

Fast forward a year later, and he is now a mentor of sorts. Our relationship evolved as we got to know each other and built a strong foundation of trust and respect. He tells me when I'm doing great things and doing something dumb. He puts me in front of the right people and lets me know which people are not necessarily worth the effort or time. He pushes me to grow personally and professionally.

Hiring a coach will change the trajectory of your business no matter what business you are in. I'm not just saying this because I am a coach. Think about it this way: At some point, all doctors need to see a doctor, many psychologists have their own therapists, dentists should go to another dentist, and as a coach, I have benefited immensely from working with other coaches. Don't wait, and don't hesitate. It's the most significant investment you'll ever make in yourself.

ABOUT THE AUTHOR

Tonya Baynes is a dynamic and skilled life coach, workplace coach, facilitator, and entrepreneur. With over a decade of coaching experience, she is passionate about guiding people to personal and professional success through targeted coaching and training programs.

Over the years, Tonya has helped individuals from diverse backgrounds and varying stages of life as a life coach.

Specializing in values identification, increased self-awareness, and goal setting, she empowers clients to overcome obstacles while growing into their authentic selves. As a workplace coach, Tonya collaborates with organizations to create positive and productive cultures. Her direct work with teams and leadership has consistently augmented employee satisfaction and retention.

Tonya is a skilled, hands-on, and engaging facilitator. Through thoughtfully curated workshops, unique events, coaching exercises, and planning sessions, she brings people together to create a shared vision for success.

An entrepreneur, Tonya has launched a coaching company, networking venture and founded a non-profit benefiting African women entrepreneurs. Her leadership, strategic partnerships, and exceptional customer service distinguish her as a respected business leader and a valuable asset to the personal and professional development community.

DIONNE TUPLIN

Tip 1: Believe in yourself!

"What business do I have running a business?"

"What if I fail?"

"Who'd listen to me?"

"I'm just a mom. What do I have to offer to the marketplace?"

Have you ever asked yourself questions like these? Believe it or not, I asked these very questions of myself when I first decided to step into the business world as an entrepreneur. I didn't think I had any business being in business. I mean, I'm a stay-at-home mom! Really?

While I had some experience in the corporate world, I left because I felt trapped and didn't see any opportunity for advancement. I *love* being a mom. I was born to be a mom, and I am pretty damn good at it. I put my all into raising my four kids to become an asset to the world, and they are my world. I also knew that I yearned for more. There was always this other desire burning within that was looking to emerge.

But I was afraid.

Old man fear kept rearing its ugly head, sprinkling little seeds of doubt, pulling me back each time I wanted to take that leap.

What I came to realize was that it was okay to be afraid and even okay to have these questions and doubts. On the other side, every fear, worry, and doubt were those things I'd wanted to do, waiting for me to take that next step.

I flipped those questions around and turned them into questions of possibility and hope. I knew that as a mom, my kids were always watching me, and if they saw me having doubts about stepping into my greatness and playing small, they would do and act the same way.

Miss Rosie Marie Jones was my third-grade teacher. I loved that woman because she was one of the first teachers who gave me my first taste of leadership. She would decorate her room for a specific month and call on a select few students to stay behind during recess to set up the room. I was ecstatic when she chose me. She saw me as someone worthy of the job. She believed in me, and during that year, she also looked to me to take care of other tasks. If she believed in me back then, I had to start believing in myself more. Sometimes all it takes is one person to inject that little something to give you the push you need. Miss Jones was that person for me.

I started to look at my strengths and where I shine. I looked at how I overcome obstacles and can find solutions that work. I'm a self-starter; when I see a need, I look for a way to fill it. You have it in you to be the best version of yourself for the world. You are important; you matter to this world, and you are here to make a difference. Believe in what you want to accomplish, look within and step into your greatness. You are amazing!

Tip 2: Make personal development your friend

"Formal education will make you a living; self-education will make you a fortune."

—Jim Rohn

I've always loved school and learning. I discovered things about myself that I didn't even know existed. I valued the friendships and leadership opportunities I was given, especially during my college days. However, I'm not very book smart. I didn't graduate with top academic honors but I always valued my time in school.

Following graduation, it was a challenge to find work. I was either overqualified or not the right fit for any positions I applied for. One company suggested that I become an entrepreneur and start my own business.

I believe that was my first real introduction to entrepreneurship, but I wasn't sure how to go about it. Where do I start? What should I do? What the heck is personal development anyway?

I was introduced to personal development in 1998 after attending a seminar for a direct-selling company. While they weren't the best fit for me, I was recommended to read Napoleon Hill's *Think and Grow Rich*.

I left that company and thought, "Eh. I'll pass on the book."

It wasn't until after I became a wife and mother that I truly delved into personal development. This was a whole new world that opened doors for me. I could learn from mentors and experts who have gone through the journey and return with all the tools needed to help me grow. The big bonus was that I could do this on time, not according to a preselected schedule that made me uncomfortable.

And the best part is that you can and should rinse and repeat those training sessions as you grow. Personal development is not one-and-done; it's a constant cycle of daily learning, growing, and improving.

I will take a different approach to personal development benefits and dive into one area that I am working on mastering: the concept of NET = No Extra Time. No Extra Time (NET) is when you anchor personal development to something you already do. While driving, instead of listening to the radio, pop in a personal development CD, listen to a podcast, an audiobook, or something that feeds your mind the fuel you need to help you grow. The time in the car is going to pass. Why not use it to grow as a person? I make my vehicle my mobile classroom. When I'm home, aside from the time that I have blocked off for work, when I'm cooking or cleaning, I'll have some sort of personal development lesson playing. NET has allowed me to incorporate personal development into my daily activities and routines. We all have the same 24/7/365, and how you use that time will make all the difference.

As for *Think and Grow Rich*, it has been part of my library for the past fifteen years, and I return to it every year.

Tip 3: Being an introvert has its benefits

Introvert (noun): "a person whose personality is characterized by introversion: a typically reserved or quiet person who tends to be introspective and enjoys spending time alone."

–Merriam-Webster Dictionary

I have come to embrace and love being an introvert. I've always been surrounded by extroverts who dominate conversations, can walk into a room, and everyone gravitates to them. I'm the one you'd find in the corner at a party or event trying to find the nearest exit.

It wasn't until the pandemic that I truly valued and embraced my introversion. Being on lockdown and not inter-acting with people and staying in our homes? Yes, please, and thank you. Finally, the world understands what it's like to be me. I realized I was living under other people's ideals of success and felt suffocated. The lockdown allowed me to evaluate my time, who I surrounded myself with, and how I wanted to learn, grow, and succeed. It all came down to me. It was always my choice, and now I could choose without guilt or worry.

My solitude is my solace. My best ideas come, and I perform better with assignments when I am alone. Give me the task, tell me when it's due, then let me be. As I'm writing this tip, it's 4:15 on a Sunday morning, everyone is asleep, and I am free from distraction to get this done. This time alone allows me to go deep with my thoughts and think things through.

I'm not necessarily shy, per se. I prefer observing and taking in conversations; when I need to share, I will. Usually, I will reach out to a person privately and start conversations. I am willing to go first (I credit my small stint with Improv as a contributing factor), but for the most part, I take in all the information, process things and ask all the possible questions and outcomes that could happen.

Relationships mean the world to me, and when you are in my inner circle, you have me for life. I am loyal to the end; I take friendships seriously and am a great listener. I'm the one people tend to share their deepest thoughts with because I'll usually let you talk.

These qualities (and many others too great to list here) have weaved into me, taking on leadership roles and shining my way without reservation. A former colleague shared that I was great to work with because I "would meet people where they are. You'd give me an assignment, let me know the deadline, and let me go. You'd check in occasionally but allowed me to do my work and submit it when it was due."

To my fellow introverts, look for those qualities that make you shine and let them work to your advantage. You know best how you operate. Don't let others try to fit you into their box. I am unapologetically embracing my introversion and loving myself more because of it.

Lesson Learned: Asking for help

In my mind, asking for help is a sign of weakness.

Putting this out there right from the beginning puts me on task.

Why would I need help? I know what needs to get done, so just do it, right? Why burden others with problems that I should be able to solve? People have enough on their plates, so why add more?

From the outside looking in, you might think, "That's ridiculous. Asking for help shows strength and courage. Everyone needs help at some point. We can't be good at everything." As I said, in my mind, I see this as the opposite, even though I know it's ridiculous.

So, where does this come from? There's always a root cause to one's thinking, right? Well, I'm no different. As far as I can remember, I've been a problem solver and would figure things out. If something were out of sorts, I would find a solution, no matter how "out there" it may seem to others. I learned by watching what others would do, and if I saw it enough times, I would mimic what I saw.

When I was five and living in California, my aunt played the piano. She practiced a tune called "Ghost Song" and played it daily. One day, when she was done on the piano, I figured I'd heard it enough times and wanted to see if I could play the song. I hopped on the seat and started playing most of what I remembered. The family thought it was my aunt, so everyone was quite shocked when they saw it was me. I even recorded myself once playing "Ghost Song" and still hear the tune in my mind.

As I got older, when it came to the basics, if something was out of sorts and there was an alternative, I'd choose it. Growing up in Brooklyn, New York, I took public transportation in high school and traveled by a couple of buses. The buses were often overcrowded, and the commute was a nightmare, but this was how I got to school. One day, I left school and was taking the buses home. I got off at Flatbush Ave and Kings Highway, waiting for my transfer bus home. Sometimes, if those buses were overcrowded, they became express buses and wouldn't stop to pick up any other passengers. That day, I had enough, and instead of waiting for the next available bus, which would most likely be overcrowded, I decided to walk home. Ignoring the fact that I was about five miles away from home, in my mind, I'd been on enough overcrowded buses and figured walking was better.

Fast forward to motherhood. For about ten years, I was a part-time single mom because my husband would travel to the western part of Canada for work and be gone for months at a time. At first, it was me and one child; I'd figure out a routine and do the best with what I had. Then we had three more kids, and a new cycle of figuring things out would begin, and we developed a routine. The kids and I stayed on PEI, and I held down the fort at home. I was the caregiver and took care of the bills, home maintenance, and everything and anything that came up. When hubby was home, he'd be home for a week, then head back out West, and the cycle would begin again. My mother-in-law lived across the street and helped out as much as possible, but for the most part, I held down the fort. No matter the challenges, the goal was to get my husband home and be a family.

Part of me is also very stubborn and set in my ways, so asking for help is a struggle. There have been times when I asked for help, and the responses were not very welcoming. Responses included eye rolls, sighs of irritation, and some nos. So, in my mind, I would equate asking for help as being a burden to others and keep the asking to a minimum. I would go back to figuring things out independently, learning from my mistakes, developing a routine, and making things work. The other side to this coin is that this way of life became second nature for me when my husband finally decided to stay home and work locally. I didn't want to give up this routine. As much as he tried to help, my mindset was still on being a part-time single parent and doing things independently.

This wasn't good for me mentally because I kept my feelings to myself, pretending everything was okay and I would run on this hamster wheel which got me nowhere. Keeping those feelings suppressed also ran the risk of imploding and lashing out at people who didn't deserve it, including my husband and kids. If I needed help, I would only ask in dire emergencies. Even then, I would feel guilty for asking, giving people an out, and continuing to do things myself.

How does this translate into the business world for me? Asking for help is still very much a struggle. If I am the one trying to figure things out and not ask for help, it will take me longer to reach my goals and build the life I seek for my family and our future. I know my strengths and my personal development journey has helped me to grow as a person. One of the areas I am working on mastering is vulnerability. I have to be willing to delegate, diminish or delete tasks where others excel and realize that asking for help benefits me and those who are eager to help.

Knowing what I know now, my focus needs to be on shifting my mindset of being the one to do it all because I can't. No one can. I have to:

1. Be more willing to give up controlling everything around me.

2. Ask for help when I am struggling.

3. Allow others to step in and help where they excel

4. Keep my focus on where I excel

5. Repeat this process over and over

I am a work in progress. Looking to the future, I want to make a global impact, which requires much help. I am slowly chipping away at being in control by showing my vulnerability, having a core group of associations who lift me up, and developing a great team of leaders who see that vision and will work diligently to make this happen. I'm excited about this venture and cannot wait to see this come to fruition.

ABOUT THE AUTHOR

Dionne Tuplin, reformed corporate lackey turned anti-latch-key kids advocate, founded M.O.M. Biz Empire. She teaches how to live a life of wellness without breaking the budget by making small, simple lifestyle changes. Her organization inspires thousands of Members on a Mission by encouraging others through articles, live streaming, and events.

Dionne's talks are designed to show how to positively use structure, discipline, and resistance to instant gratification. Dionne demonstrates how now is the time to teach children to be true to themselves, show empathy for others, and keep family values as the core.

On stage, you'll feel how Dionne is real and quiet but has a bold message, teaching audiences practical strategies with immediate and long-term impact. Dionne has spoken to executives, entrepreneurs, and stay-at-home moms.

Dionne was born in Jamaica, raised in New York, and lives with her family on Prince Edward Island in Canada. She graduated from St. John's University with a B.A. in Sociology. As a jovial Jamaican, Dionne won't jerk you around, and she makes the meanest jerk chicken you've ever tasted!

SHAWN HUBER

Tip 1: The Power of Balance: Thriving in Life and Business

The journey towards greatness commences even before your birth as you embark on continuous learning. From the moment you enter this world, a torrent of information surrounds you, shaping your unique personality with its preferences and aversions. As you grow, formal education takes center stage, providing the foundation to explore and discover the subjects that captivate your heart. Becoming the go-to expert in your chosen field is exhilarating, but how do you share your knowledge with the rest of the world?

Consistency is the key. You can break free from the confines of limited exposure by consistently sharing your expertise through means that resonate with you. Embrace every opportunity to spread your passion without burning out, entrusting the rest to the experts. Building a balanced system that allows you to focus on what only you can do is crucial. However, it requires a support system that empowers you to share your message effectively.

In my own life, I have faced tremendous challenges while running a business. Let me take you back to 2005 when I underwent a routine surgery, unaware of the life-altering diagnosis it would unveil. Cancer. The shock was overwhelming, but I confronted the situation head-on, armed with resilience and determination. This part of my journey taught me invaluable lessons and revealed the true power of assembling a strong team.

When I mention a team, you may envision those who work within your business. But I encourage you to think bigger. Your support system extends far beyond the confines of your organization. My team included exceptional individuals, such as Larry Einhorn, renowned as Lance Armstrong's doctor. Larry's expertise and unwavering commitment to my well-being became an inspiration. His involvement reinforced the importance of having the best team members by your side.

Larry designed a rigorous protocol tailored to my needs—five days a week of eight-hour IV chemotherapy sessions, followed by one week off, and then back to the grueling routine again. The dedication of Larry, his team, and my larger support system is precisely why I am still here today, sharing my message.

Now, I want you to pause momentarily and ask yourself, *Who's on my team?* Take time to assess if you have the support system necessary to help you focus on sharing your expertise on a large scale. Your team comprises individuals who care about your well-being, both personally and professionally. Some members may focus on your health, ensuring you have the strength and vitality to pursue your dreams. Others will assist you in reaching even more people with your message, expanding your influence and impact. Remember, you cannot do this alone.

Reflect on the individuals who have consistently supported you throughout your journey. Are they the right people to have by your side as you strive for greatness? Consider the qualities and expertise they bring to the table. Nurture those relationships, cultivate new ones, and seek out those with the skills and insights that complement your own.

Your team extends beyond your immediate circle; it includes mentors, coaches, experts, and collaborators. Embrace the strength that comes from collaboration and leverage the collective power of a well-rounded team. Together, you can accomplish far more than you ever could alone.

So, ask yourself again, "Who's on my team?" Commit to building a support system that empowers you to share your expertise boldly, passionately, and on a grand scale. Remember that your experiences shape you, making you stronger and more tenacious as an entrepreneur. Embrace the power of your team, for they are the ones who will uplift you, champion your cause, and help you unleash your full potential. Let their unwavering support propel you toward greatness.

Tip 2: The Power of Teamwork: Building a Support System for Success

Doing more doesn't automatically guarantee success in your business or personal life. Pushing yourself beyond your limits can harm your well-being and overall success. There's a threshold for how much stress your mind and body can handle daily; exceeding that limit leads to burnout. However, there is a way to condition yourself to handle more without sacrificing your health or happiness. It begins with establishing systems that aid recovery and creating a daily routine prioritizing all aspects of your life.

Stress is a complex phenomenon that encompasses both positive and negative factors. It's not inherently wrong, but it needs to be balanced. To counterbalance the stressors in your life, you must implement a holistic approach that includes other crucial areas of your life, such as hobbies, family and friends, personal care, spirituality, and your mission. It's not just about striving for more money or a bigger business; it's about achieving holistic success and finding fulfillment in all aspects of your life. By improving and nurturing these areas, you can generate more wealth while reducing the need for a constant hustle-and-grind mentality.

Here's a simple system to guide you on this journey. Take a moment to rate yourself from one to ten in the following areas: finances, friendship and family, hobbies, spirituality, mission, and health. Pay particular attention to the areas with lower ratings, which indicate areas where you may need more time and energy. However, remember that your attitude is key to the success of this system—it must remain positive. Consistent implementation of this approach will make remarkable improvements in all areas of your life. While the process may be simple, it requires dedication and commitment to execute consistently.

Life is filled with stressors, both expected and unexpected. How you handle these stressors is what truly matters. Being diagnosed with cancer has been one of the most stressful events in my life. During this challenging time, one of my business partners took advantage of the donated funds intended to assist me during my financial struggles. Instead of using the money as planned, he selfishly diverted it to cover his personal expenses. The shocking part was that he was completely unaware of the actual amount that had been donated. I only discovered this unfortunate truth when I inquired about it. Engaging in a fight or argument over this matter was the last thing I needed while undergoing treatment. The stress caused by this situation was detrimental to my overall well-being.

To cope with this additional stress, I focused on maintaining a clean and nourishing diet, engaging in moderate exercise, and taking supplements to support my body's resilience. These practices were essential in keeping my stress levels as low as possible while undergoing treatment. Additionally, I decided to continue working during the initial phase of my treatment, which introduced even more stress into my life. However, I did receive a small portion of the business profits during my absence. Now here's the remarkable part—when I returned to work after a four-month break, I emerged as the second-highest earner among the four partners that year. This achievement was significant because it highlighted the power of prioritizing how I handled my stress and the strength that can come from overcoming it.

This story serves as a reminder that stress and adversity are inevitable in life, but how we navigate through them defines our success. By prioritizing your well-being and implementing strategies to manage stress, you can overcome challenges and thrive. Remember that you can bounce back stronger, even after setbacks and difficult circumstances.

As you embark on your journey toward balance and success, remember to embrace the power of a holistic approach. Nurture all areas of your life, create systems that aid your recovery, and prioritize self-care. Doing so will unlock your full potential, achieve remarkable results, and create a fulfilling life and business that go hand in hand.

Tip 3: Teambuilding extends to people outside of your business staff

Years after my battle with cancer, my current wife and I were told that we had a zero percent chance of conceiving a child. Despite this discouraging prognosis, we refused to let others dictate our limits. With the right mindset and unwavering support from our team, we defied the odds. Through a combination of supplements, modern medicine, and an unyielding belief in the possibility of miracles, my wife became pregnant, and our beautiful daughter was born the following September. This experience reinforced the importance of believing in what is possible and assembling the right team for you.

At the time, I was a personal trainer faced with demanding work hours that often stretched from early morning to late evening. At the same time, my wife, who was a teacher, decided to transition into coaching, which required time and effort to establish a new income stream. The pressure to support our family fell primarily on my shoulders during those initial years. Juggling a demanding career and the responsibilities of parenthood tested our resilience. However, with the support of our team, including friends and mentors, we navigated the ups and downs and gradually built a foundation for success. Support played a vital role in helping each team member develop new skills and contribute to our collective growth.

Your team is the most important aspect of your journey in life and business. Family, mentors, friends, business partners, and employees are just some of the people who could make up your team.

Your team has the power to lift you up and run alongside you until you reach your goal. I discovered the true strength of teamwork when I participated in a Tough Mudder race. If you're unfamiliar with Tough Mudder, it's an intense team event that challenges physical and mental endurance. While I wasn't an experienced long-distance runner, I decided to take on the challenge. However, doubts crept in the night before the race, and I considered backing out. My team, composed of high school friends, inspired me to push forward and not let them down. Little did I know that this race would test not only my physical capabilities but also the strength of our teamwork.

The race took place on a vast hunting ranch, with thousands of participants tackling a grueling course of twelve miles and twenty-four intense obstacles. I pushed myself to overcome most challenges, but my body gave in to severe cramps and exhaustion at mile eight. Attempting to clear a hay bale obstacle, my knee gave way, forcing me to seek medical assistance. It was humbling as I had been so focused on supporting my team that I neglected to ask for help when needed. The medics participating in the race rushed to my aid, and I was unable to continue the course. My team completed the race without me, and it was then that my wife, who had been waiting at the finish line, sensed something was wrong.

I went into shock in the medical tent, and my wife quickly found me amidst the sea of participants. We rushed to a nearby emergency hospital, where a doctor confirmed significant damage to my knee. During those critical days, I relied on friends for support, as my scheduled friend did not show up as planned. The physical and emotional toll of the experience was immense, but it highlighted the importance of team members being aware of each other's struggles and stepping in when needed. We must understand our limitations, ask for help, and say no when we're overwhelmed. Through this mutual support and understanding, we can overcome obstacles and grow stronger as a team.

Lesson Learned: The Path to Greatness: Knowledge, Balance, and Teamwork

Building your team goes beyond assembling individuals who work inside your business. It encompasses all areas of your life, including family, friends, mentors, and experts in their respective fields. Take the time to identify your strengths and weaknesses and seek the necessary support to improve in all aspects. Learn from those who have achieved what you aspire to do and strive to excel even further. Maintain a positive attitude, and choose activities that bring you joy, as your emotional state is your responsibility. Embrace failure, overcome tragedy, and celebrate remarkable accomplishments; they are all part of life's journey. Strive to become a better version of yourself daily, teach and serve others to the best of your abilities, and pursue your dreams with unwavering determination.

Remember, success is not a solo endeavor but a team effort. Surround yourself with a supportive network, nurture those relationships, and uplift one another on the path to greatness. Together, you can overcome any challenge, achieve remarkable results, and create a life and business that flourish in harmony.

So, what does all of this have to do with business? Life teaches us numerous lessons, and building our lives as the central focus is important, with everything else revolving around it. Your team begins with you. Take the time to identify your strengths and weaknesses in all areas of life. Seek the necessary support to improve in all aspects. Follow the lead of those who have achieved what you aspire to and strive to do it even better. Maintain a positive attitude and choose what brings you joy, as your emotional state is your responsibility. Failure, tragedy, and extraordinary accomplishments are all part of life. Strive to become a better version of yourself every day and teach and serve others to the best of your abilities. Do this because it is the right thing to do.

ABOUT THE AUTHOR

Shawn Huber is a Certified High Performance Coach with the High Performance Institute and Certified Medical Hypnotherapist. He founded Structured Freedom, a Transformational Coaching company that guides people to connect their minds and body to become healthier. Shawn believes that by having a plan, people can achieve their goals and dreams and have the freedom to live the life they desire.

Shawn has over fifteen years of coaching experience and has worked with a diverse range of clients that all have a common goal of making positive changes to go from "Good to Great." Remember who is in charge and make it happen.

ARMED WITH TIPS, NOW WHAT?

This book is chock-full of tips from highly talented and experienced entrepreneurs and business owners.

The motivation behind writing this book and publishing it was straightforward—to help you get where you want to go with less pain in less time.

Now you have to decide if you will follow the advice and put in the work necessary to succeed. There is no substitute for sweat equity.

We all hope you will dig into the opportunities you seek, armed with our guidance, and push past the resistance into prosperity.

I recommend you keep this book at arm's length and return to it as often as needed. The difference between knowledge and wisdom is how you apply what you learn along your journey.

Thank you for reading *Business Tips From The Trenches: Expert Advice to Start Your Small Business or Side Hustle.*

If you love the book, please leave us a positive review on Amazon and let your friends know that you recommend they pick up a copy and read it.

Bowman Digital Media
Ira Bowman
SEO Specialist

951-902-9550

ira@bowmandigitalmedia.com

What We Do

Increase sales by generating more website traffic

How We Help

SEO
Search Engine Optimization includes content creation, backlink building, metadata, keyword and traffic monitoring

Website Development and Maintenance
We are WordPress developers

Graphic Design
For Print or Online - Logos, Business Cards, Brochures, Custom Design Work

Photography
Headshots, Event, Product, and Lifestyle

Videography
Video Shooting and Editing

Social Media Marketing
All platforms including: LinkedIn, Facebook, Instagram, YouTube, Pinterest, Twitter, and more.

Sales Growth by Design

www.bowmandigitalmedia.com